I believe replanting a church is ~~...~~ ... the most strategic ways to push back darkness and advance the kingdom of God. Mark Clifton has the experience, the passion, and the data to help us reach North America through the local church.

Darrin Patrick, author of *Replant* and lead pastor,
The Journey, St. Louis, Missouri

I've known Mark Clifton for longer than either of us would like to admit. In those years, I have often turned to him for direction and advice—and he's consistently delivered at key points along the way. Now, I'm thrilled that you get to benefit from the advice I've received for years. In *Reclaiming Glory*, Mark points us to a better future to restarted churches—where the work of God continues in the facility that belonged to the Lord all along. I'm grateful for Mark and his advice—and grateful that you now have access to both!

Ed Stetzer, president of LifeWay Research, LifeWay
Christian Resources, www.edstetzer.com

I personally know one no one more qualified or passionate about "replanting" than Mark Clifton. He writes both from wisdom and experience in *Reclaiming Glory* in dying churches. Your HOPE will rise as you read of stories of vision and victory.

Johnny Hunt, pastor, First Baptist Church,
Woodstock, Georgia

In recent days there has been a church-planting movement gaining momentum across North America. Many of God's finest servants have devoted themselves to this noble undertaking. But now a new movement is surging that focuses on replanting existing churches. This could be the spark that ignites revival in America. Mark Clifton has successfully planted and replanted churches. He knows what he is talking about. I am so excited about his new book!

Richard Blackaby, president,
Blackaby Ministries International and author
of *Flickering Lamps* and *Experiencing God*

The landscape of North America is littered with empty church buildings and dwindling congregations. I praise God for raising up Mark Clifton, who has been a voice crying in the wilderness, seeking to reverse these trends. In addition to presenting this helpful resource, Clifton has a proven track record of seeking and bringing about renewal in dying congregations. Every person who loves the local church will benefit from reading *Reclaiming Glory*, and those who find themselves about the hard work of revitalizing a struggling congregation should put this book on the top of their reading list.

Jason K. Allen, president,
Midwestern Baptist Theological Seminary

Mark Clifton loves the church and he has a passion for stories of rebirth—especially when it means bringing a dying church back to vitality and biblical relevance once again by replanting it. Hundreds of our churches die each year. Thousands of church buildings now serve as bookstores, art galleries, coffee shops, or simply stand empty. It is not an easy process, but every one of us should want to see this sad trend end and Mark lays out the plan within these pages. Let's do all we can to see that God's churches reflect and proclaim his glory once again.

Kevin Ezell, president,
North American Mission Board, SBC

This is an essential read for all church leaders and members who are wanting to see their church spring to life again! Mark is a proven practitioner whom God has used effectively to do what he is writing about. This book is a boots on the ground, trench warfare manual for doing the work of revitalization, replanting, or just flat-out rescuing.

Andy Addis, lead pastor, CrossPoint Church,
Hutchinson, Kansas

I love the established church. Aside from a year planting churches in Africa, my entire ministry has been invested in older, established churches. It is exciting to me, then, every time I hear Mark Clifton communicate his vision for seeing a national renewal for declining churches. This book is so good because it is birthed not just in Mark's passion, but in his experience. If you love the church and want to see declining churches thrive again, you really need to read this book.

Micah Fries, VP of LifeWay Research,
LifeWay Christian Resources

Church revitalization is such a unique, hard, and noble work that it cannot be learned rightly from a scholar who has merely theorized about it, but must be learned from someone who has lived it, done it, and has the scars to show it. Mark Clifton is that seasoned, proven teacher and his book, *Reclaiming Glory* confirms his strong and credible voice. In this book, you will find a treasure of wise, thoughtful, biblical, and practical tools to understand the importance of this work and how to be engage in it so that the gospel is magnified and God is glorified. Every pastor needs to read this book. I highly commend it!

Brian Croft, senior pastor, Auburndale
Baptist Church in Louisville, Kentucy, and
senior fellow for the Mathena Center for Church
Revitalization at Southern Seminary

In his work *Reclaiming Glory*, Mark Clifton outlines the gospel initiative of reclaiming dying churches for the purpose of kingdom advancement. His pathways for replanting show strategic thought in genuine considerations which should be engaged. No one wants to see a church close its doors. However, if one gets to this point, there are ways to reclaim the preaching point for the purpose of continuing the story of Jesus in a community. A needed resource for needed conversations in our churches today.

Kenneth Priest, director, Convention Strategies,
Southern Baptists of Texas Convention

RECLAIMING
GLORY

RECLAIMING
GLORY

REVITALIZING **DYING** CHURCHES

MARK**CLIFTON**

B&H
PUBLISHING GROUP
NASHVILLE, TENNESSEE

978-1-4336-4322-4

Published by B&H Publishing Group
Nashville, Tennessee

Dewey Decimal Classification: 254.5
Subject Heading: CHURCH RENEWAL \ CHURCH
GROWTH \ LEADERSHIP

1 2 3 4 5 6 7 • 21 20 19 18 17 16

This book is dedicated to my dad, Harry Clifton, a loving dad, preacher of the gospel, and compassionate pastor for more than sixty years. God used my dad's deep and abiding love of the local church with all of her blemishes to instill in me a calling to reclaim dying churches.

ACKNOWLEDGMENTS

This book would not have been possible without many people investing in my life and ministry. First among those is my wife, Jill. She is the epitome of a replant pastor's wife. Jill possesses in abundance the key quality required of a replanter's wife: spousal perseverance. She is a constant encourager and my dearest friend in all the world.

I will always be thankful to the dear saints that are the Wornall Road Baptist Church in Kansas City, Missouri, where my understanding and passion for replanting was developed. God used the young pastors at Wornall to shape me for my fourth-quarter ministry.

Much of the research and information contained in this book was a result of a collaboration with a great group of replanting pastors: Bob Bickford, Mark Hallock, Josh King, Brad O'Brien, Nathan Rose, and Adam Wyatt. These are some of the boldest soldiers of the gospel that I have ever known.

CONTENTS

FOREWORD

Over the past four decades, one untested yet habitually echoed axiom has garnered an almost biblical standing in our evangelical easy-speak: *healthy churches grow*. The unspoken implication is that if a church is healthy, it has an infinite upward trajectory.

It seems that despite both the evidence of church history and the overwhelming weight of self-sacrificial kingdom themes within Scripture—it all really comes down to this singular all-important metric: *do we have more sitting in our sacred pews this year than last?* If not, the school of church growth's rubrics indicate momentous internal and unnatural problems.

For the majority of evangelicals, this new dogma is not an emboldening creed.

Study after study indicates that 70 to 80 percent of evangelical churches in North America are either plateaued or declining.

Like other organisms, churches tend to grow fastest in the earliest stages, reproduce frequently during their maturing years and hopefully assist as wise, generous, and loving grandparents during their final years.

It's tragic that so many churches do just the opposite to what they are eternally designed to do. When we start to plateau, rather than seeking a kingdom legacy, we often turn inward and frantically concentrate on our own growth. Aging churches often choose the sterility of "saving itself" over the exponential advance of the kingdom of God.

That leads us back to our problem. With 70 to 80 percent of our churches in a state of plateau or decline, what are our options? Three biblical themes should serve as a guide:

- Remember. Remember all the ways God has used this church to expand His kingdom. Recall the faces and families that have been unmistakably impacted by the faithfulness of your witness. Perhaps remembering the past will serve as a re-tracking for the future. Revelation 2:5 instructs us to remember and repeat the earlier things.

- Remember Kingdom. No cold cup of water offered humbly in Jesus' name is without eternal impact. Think of how King Jesus might use the resources and wisdom with which he has blessed you for increased kingdom impact.

The lore of church growth tells us that we are corporate failures if we are unable to produce winning numbers. The King of the kingdom tells us that true kingdom fruit is found in an open-handed posture of selflessness.

"Truly, truly, I say to you, unless a grain of wheat falls into the earth and dies, it remains alone; but if it dies, it bears much fruit" (John 12:24).

- Remember Multiplication. How might you bear much fruit? Certainly not by going down grasping clenched-fisted as a dead-end link on the Great Commission chain. We never bear fruit by "saving ourselves." It emerges simply through the spiritual abandonment of "losing ourselves." What about our legacy of multiplication? It is the assignment to which God has called his church.

Do healthy churches continually grow? The evidence for our first 2000 years would lead us to an unequivocal "No. "

What theology does a dying and self-absorbed church broadcast to its community? What eternal questions does it inspire? Likely not, "Can they help me with me with my life's deepest troubles?"

Imagine a different future. Imagine a church approaching the end of its physical life cycle that is captivated with the priority of being a living demonstration of God's glory incarnate in its community. With open hands it sacrifices its preferences, resources, and even its organizational structures for a lasting kingdom legacy. In the death of these things a curious community is witness to the vibrant life and glory of Jesus Christ rising up in their very midst. The kingdom of God is powerfully advanced by the people of God prizing the reputation of Christ over the fading relic of their brand.

Does "plateaued or declining" mean little or no kingdom impact? It all depends on whose church it is.

Over the next chapters, Mark Clifton, will inspire us to consider pursuing God's glory over our own. He will challenge us to reflect on the legacy that our churches will ultimately be leaving; either one that stands the test of eternity, or one that further exacerbates evangelical mediocrity through misdirected self-worship.

May God use this book to inspire kingdom priorities among the lives of the people of God who have long served him well.

Jeff Christopherson
Milton, Georgia

CHAPTER 1

NEW LIFE FOR DYING CHURCHES

Most of us who call Kansas City home will not soon forget November 3, 2015. That's because we were nearly all together for one of the most unlikely events in the city's history. An estimated eight hundred thousand people packed the parade route to celebrate the recently crowned World Series champion Kansas City Royals. That's nearly double the population of our city (and roughly 9 percent of the total population of the states of Missouri and Kansas). School was cancelled so that the children could attend the parade. For the first time in thirty years the second smallest market in Major League Baseball won the sport's greatest prize. A year after the Royals lost in dramatic fashion—with the tying run of game seven of the World Series just ninety feet away—the Comeback Kids finished the deal with an epic four-games-to-one defeat of the Mets. And on November 3, the city came out to celebrate. Just a few years earlier, that parade would have been unfathomable.

For a decade, from 1976 to 1985, the Royals were one of the dominant teams in baseball. Seven times in ten years they went to the play-offs. Thanks to a future Hall of Famer, George Brett, and a great cast of supporting players, they were relevant nearly every year—including winning two American League pennants and a World Series title in 1985. But, until their 2014 play-off run, the last time the Royals even made the play-offs had been nearly thirty years earlier. That was the longest play-off drought of any team in any major sport.

But the Kansas City Royals' title run in 2015 almost never happened. In 2002 Major League Baseball's owners, looking to shore up the sport's shaky financial situation, actively discussed the possibility of disbanding two teams. The Royals were among the teams rumored to be on the list.

Who would have blamed owners if they had done it? The Royals were at the tail end of eight consecutive losing seasons. In 2002 only three teams drew fewer fans. Only eight teams had lower player payrolls. The Royals looked done in 2002.

But the Royals didn't die, and in 2015 they wrote a new, exciting chapter in franchise history. Fan attendance is now up. According to a May 2015 *New York Times* article, television viewership is up four times where it was five years ago. And the team that once was the laughingstock of baseball has a higher television rating than any other team in baseball. At one point early in 2015, the Royals had eight players on track to being voted All Stars by Major League Baseball fans. (Four were eventually voted into the game by the fans.) That would have been unfathomable a decade earlier. Considering the age of the team's best players, the revitalized Royals appear likely to make 2015 the first of many championships to come.

Most evangelical churches in North America have much more in common with the 2002 Royals than the 2015 version. You have likely heard the depressing stats. Southern Baptists alone lose more than nine hundred churches every year. Ninety percent of those churches are in our cities. Seven out of ten churches are either plateaued or declining. They haven't seen a "winning season" in more years than they can count.

Like the Royals, the best days of many churches seem to be over. In the past when I attended Royals games, I would see the sign in the outfield celebrating the 1985 World Series championship. Rather than making me proud to be a Royals fan, that sign reminded me that greatness had not been part of this team for a long time. In the same way, when walking the halls of a dying church, one can find memories of the great days of the past. But those great days seem so long ago. Instead of serving as encouragement, those memories serve as constant reminders of how far the church has fallen.

Accepting God's call to replant a dying church is never easy. Any idea how many managers the Royals have gone through since their last play-off appearance? Ten. Losing seasons—whether in baseball or in ministry—tend to devour leaders.

But God has other plans.

Several years ago God led me to replant a dying church, Wornall Road Baptist in Kansas City, Missouri. The very few remaining members of Wornall Road made the extraordinary and all-too-rare decision to repent of past mistakes, praying with passionate focus and embracing meaningful and biblical change. Over the next few years the church began to grow. We became relevant to our community, and we planted new churches. Today Wornall has become a church to which many across North America have looked as a model of how a dying church can live again.

Wornall Road doesn't look much like the 1940s version. We don't do ministry the same way. We don't serve the community in the same manner. And we certainly don't have the same cast of leaders. But we are relevant and reaching our community once again. The power that enabled the first generation of Wornall members is again empowering this present generation—that is the power of the gospel as revealed and lived out in the lives of our members.

It's a good time to be a Royals fan, and it's a good time to replant dying churches.

The Dying-Church Dilemma

Dying churches are more critical in the realm of eternity than an underachieving baseball team, and we are facing a dying-church dilemma in North America. Every year in my denomination, the Southern Baptist Convention (SBC), nine hundred churches disappear from our rolls. Most of them just close their doors.[1] But the reality is that's just the tip of the iceberg. According to LifeWay Research statistics, only about 15 percent of SBC churches are healthy, growing, and multiplying churches. The vast majority of our churches in North America are struggling.

There are fruitless churches all across North America, churches where new disciples aren't being made and neighboring communities aren't being transformed. A church that is not producing fruit does not accurately reflect God's glory. It doesn't make much of God to the community or the nations. Even worse, many of us have stopped expecting fruit from these churches. That is tragic.

First, we must identify what it means for a church to bear fruit. What constitutes biblical success in the life of a church? The answer isn't simply to be bigger this year than last year, even if a majority of people might think otherwise.

In Matthew 28, Jesus clearly explains what he expects of his followers. As he was about to depart from this earth, he didn't ask his disciples to gather larger crowds or to raise large sums of money or to construct great buildings. He commanded us to make disciples.

"Go, therefore, and make disciples of all nations, baptizing them in the name of the Father and of the Son and of the Holy Spirit, teaching them to observe everything I have commanded you.

And remember, I am with you always, to the end of the age." (Matt. 28:19–20)

It is important that we understand how to define success as we replant churches. Success—bearing fruit in the life of a church—means having a pattern of making disciples who make disciples that results in the community being noticeably better. Pretty simple. In reality, dying churches don't primarily have an attendance problem, a giving problem, or a baptism problem. They have a discipleship problem. When a church is making disciples who make disciples, all those other issues will be addressed. Unfortunately, many churches have little understanding of real disciple-making. Discipleship isn't a program; it doesn't take place in a classroom. Discipleship is sharing life and seeking to reproduce ourselves in others.

Paul describes the nature of disciple-making in 1 Thessalonians 2:8: "We cared so much for you that we were pleased to share with you not only the gospel of God but also our own lives, because you had become dear to us."

Churches in North America are dying from a lack of disciple-making.

Andy Addis, pastor of CrossPoint Church in Hutchinson, Kansas, has replanted a church and rescued many other dying churches. Recently I heard

Andy share his insight into The Parable of the Barren Fig Tree, and it cuts to the heart of replanting.

Jesus tells a story in Luke 13 about a man who had a fig tree in his vineyard that hadn't produced fruit in three years. The vineyard owner's solution wasn't to lower the expectation of the tree. He didn't urge the vinedresser to ignore the problem and hope it would go away. He didn't offer excuses for the unfruitfulness, such as predators or unfavorable weather. His command was short and clear—*cut it down.*

I believe we can have a similar expectation when it comes to declining churches. We don't have a right to go on, year after year, never seeing disciples made in our churches. We are not entitled to our churches if they aren't bearing fruit by making disciples. Why does the owner of the vineyard command the keeper to cut down the tree? It's not out of spite or as punishment for its lack of fruit. It's because the very presence of the fruitless tree is keeping other fruit from developing. And the vineyard owner won't stand for that.

Of course, my favorite part of the parable is when the vinedresser intervenes and asks for one more year before the tree is removed. The vinedresser acknowledges he will have to break up the hard ground and add nutrients to the soil. (Why he didn't do that before is anyone's guess.) Faced with removal of the tree, the vinedresser is ready to take action. That's how it is with those who are called to replant, too. We have to break up the hard places and add nutrients to starving soil. But more of that later.

A New Perspective on an Age-Old Problem

Throughout most of my ministry, I thought I knew everything I needed to know about plateaued and declining churches, and it all could be summed up in two words: *stay away*. I had been a church planter for twenty years by the early 2000s. Like most of my church planter friends, I figured it was easier to start a new church in a school down the street than to resurrect a dying one. And honestly, I was right. *In my experience, it is easier to start a new church than to resurrect a dying one.* Then again, what's right and what's expedient are rarely the same in Jesus' economy.

My perspective on declining churches began to change in 2003 when I moved back home to Kansas City, Missouri, to become the associate director of missions at the Blue River Kansas City Baptist Association. I had been serving in Canada where we had, at the time, about 150 Southern Baptist churches stretching across six time zones. Kansas City had nearly 130 SBC churches in two counties.

Going from an area that had an immense need for new churches to one having quite a few existing, but declining, churches meant I had to determine what God wanted to do with me in my new surroundings.

It didn't take long for the struggling churches that now surrounded me to haunt me. They seemed to be everywhere. Worse yet, many of them were crowded into what is called the inner-suburban ring, areas that boomed after World War II but had transitioned in recent decades. This area needed thriving, diverse, gospel-centered churches the most, but many of these communities had no such church. Many residents in that suburban ring had never experienced healthy local neighborhood churches that were involved in the community. Every week the declining churches in their midst simply reinforced the tired narrative that most people believed: *Church is an irrelevant place where people whose lives are nothing like mine do things that have no connection to how I live my life.* For a pastor's kid who had witnessed his dad invest his life in thriving, gospel-preaching churches, this realization was devastating.

Maybe what bothered me the most is that it had become the new norm. Many pastors of these declining churches just assumed that growth was no longer possible in these places. Many denominations had given up on these churches and were putting their resources in places where they could expect "higher results." But I couldn't get one particular thought out of my head: *What about a dying church brings glory to God?*

It was a stunner for me. That question changed my life—not because of my answer to it, but because I had no answer. Nothing about a dying church gives glory to God. Strategically, it may make more sense to start something new down the street. But it seemed that allowing that church to die would bring dishonor and disrepute on the name of Jesus within that community, certainly not glory and honor.

I had never tried to turn around a struggling church. I had spent nearly my whole life getting new churches started. Still, I wondered if I could use some of the same principles I had uncovered as a church planter to help dying churches live again. I had started churches by loving and exegeting (assessing) my community, by reaching and discipling young men, by creating simple and reproducible strategies, by preaching Christ-centered, biblically sound sermons, and by covering it all with prayer.

I also knew the risks. The stakes were high. Touch a dying church, and you will likely set your ministry back years. Pastors risk their reputations, their livelihoods, and their emotional health when they get involved in struggling churches.

But only God could get the glory if he turned these churches around. Their deaths wouldn't glorify God. He wasn't interested in how easy the effort would be. He wasn't interested in my reputation as a "successful" pastor. His glory mattered more to him than anything else—and that's what should matter to me, too.

A dying church robs God of glory. Nothing matters more than his glory. Whether a church dies in Kansas City, Boston, or in rural Texas, we must care about what that church's death means in respect to the glory of God. I decided, right then and there, I would do whatever it takes to help these churches come back to life. Little did I know at the time how that decision would change my life.

A few months later I was asked to help Wornall Road Baptist Church, a church near death. God had already been working on my heart to help struggling churches. This seemed like a very practical opportunity for me to do just that. Over the next few years I began applying some of the principles to replanting Wornall Road that I had used in planting new churches for more than twenty years.

God worked a miracle in our church and in our neighborhood over the next few years. Where a decade ago sat a dying church that had a horrible reputation in our neighborhood now sits a church that is thriving and impacting its neighborhood in real and tangible ways. (You read some of this story earlier in this book, and you'll find a more complete version of it later.)

Life in the Valley of Dry Bones

I must admit, though, as I looked out at all those declining churches in Kansas City in the early 2000s, I felt much like Ezekiel must have felt when God gave him that prophetic vision of dry bones we read about in Ezekiel 37. God had given Ezekiel the unenviable task of preaching to a spiritually dried-up people who appeared to be well beyond their heyday. Just like many of us feel when we are called to places that seem parched spiritually, Ezekiel must have wondered whether preaching to "dry bones" was pointless. But God wasn't through with Israel. And God has made it crystal clear to me in the past decade that he is not through with many of the churches in our cities and towns across the continent that appear to be dying. Whether it's Israel in the sixth century BC or twenty-first-century North America, spiritually dead institutions of faith die for one reason and one reason only: they stop loving what they once loved and stop doing what they once did.

Jesus said this to the church in Ephesus in Revelation 2:

> "I know your works, your labor, and your endurance, and that you cannot tolerate evil. You have tested those who call themselves apostles and are not, and you have found them to be liars. You also possess endurance and have tolerated many things because of My name and have not grown weary. But I have this against you: You have abandoned the love you had at first. Remember then how far you have fallen; repent, and do the works you did at first." (vv. 2–5)

In this passage, the Lord makes it clear. As many have said, the pathway to new life for a dying church is *repentance* and *remembering*. Scripture isn't talking about the nostalgic kind of remembering that builds your pride through control and a desire to return to a better time. Instead the pathway to new life comes when we remember the legacy of missions and ministry that birthed the new church in the first place and become broken to return to that place once again. This kind of remembering can only happen on the other side of repentance.

That is the heartbeat of what it means to replant a church. It is the process of ensuring a continued *legacy* for the thousands of near-death churches throughout North America by leading them to reengage with the missions and ministry that laid the foundation of the church. Can you imagine what could happen if thousands of churches that are now dying across North America found new life again? Can you imagine the revival that would sweep our land? Most important, can you imagine what kind of glory that would bring the God who made us and saved us?

For the Glory of God

As followers of Jesus, we have been called to live worthy of God's glory (see 1 Cor. 10:31)—or his value or weightiness, as the term accurately means. It's an immense calling that God gives the church.

As the apostle Paul proclaims, "Now to Him who is able to do above and beyond all that we ask or think according to the power that works in us—to Him be glory in the church and in Christ Jesus to all generations, forever and ever" (Eph. 3:20–21).

The local church is a unique institution in the world where God's glory is on display to the community. When a business goes under in your neighborhood, God's glory isn't impacted as it is when a church dies. For many neighborhoods around our continent, local churches are the ever-present, physical reminders of who God is. When the church struggles, God's reputation within that community struggles. When a church dies, we must ask ourselves, "What about a dying church reflects the glory of God or the power of the cross to a hurting and confused world?" When those churches were first planted in the neighborhoods where they now reside, they staked a claim for the glory of God in those physical places in a very real way. When they die, they are also making a profound statement about God to that community.

A few times in life God brings across our paths something that causes us to make an extreme pivot. We all have those moments—sometimes a few of them. For me, one of those moments came when I was given a copy of John Piper's book *Let the Nations Be Glad!* Reading the carefully crafted first few lines of the book particularly made a profound impact on me by reminding me of a biblical principle that would soon become a foundation of my future ministry.

Piper cited Psalm 92:1 and Psalm 67:3–4 as he wrote:

Missions is not the ultimate goal of the church. Worship is. Missions exists because worship doesn't. Worship is ultimate, not missions, because God is ultimate, not man. When this age is over, and the countless millions of the redeemed fall on their faces before the throne of God, missions will be no more. It is a temporary necessity. But worship abides forever. Worship, therefore, is the fuel and goal of missions. It's the goal of missions because in missions we simply aim to bring the nations into the white hot enjoyment of God's glory. The goal of missions is the gladness of the peoples in the greatness of God.[2]

Those words still stir my heart today, fifteen years after I first read them. I had been a pastor and a church-planting missionary for nearly twenty years by that point. The primary motivation for my work had been reaching people with the gospel. While that's an important, noble goal for any missionary or minister of the gospel, it was those words that started me on a journey to examine why we do what we do.

More than fifty times in Scripture, God makes it abundantly clear that everything, including us and his church, were created for his glory. In Matthew 5:16 Jesus gives us a primary motivation for replanting dying churches, "In the same way, let your light shine before men, so that they may see your good works and give glory to your Father in heaven." We replant churches because we want people to see what God is doing in our lives. We want people to see how lives transformed by and covenanting together for the gospel can have positive impact on a community. We want people to see in our lives the glory of the gospel. We replant churches to reclaim God's glory in a tangible way in our communities.

The Only Motivation That Matters

As I have already said, it's often easier to close a dying church and go across the street to plant a new one than it is to replant. At a new church plant you don't have to worry about the baggage from previous leaders. You don't have to navigate through an often complicated change process. You don't have to spend time with longtime members whose hearts have grown cold to the gospel. But when you replant a dying church, you have to do all of those hard things and many more. Yet once accomplished, it becomes a platform to display God's glory. You give people a living picture of what the gospel looks like—*what was once dead is now alive.*

We can tend to have many different motivations for replanting dying churches. Sometimes it's just about survival. We want the church building that contains so many warm memories to breathe with new life. We simply long for a time we perceived to have been better. As Ed Stetzer so correctly said, "Nostalgia is a cul-de-sac. It leads nowhere."[3]

Other times it's our ego. We want to prove to the world, and maybe to ourselves, that we can turn this church around. And at still other times, our reason is biblical, evangelistic, and compassionate. We want to see people in our neighborhoods come to faith in Jesus. Of course we do, and we should. But I would suggest that even that noble desire may not be sustainable over the length of time it takes to replant. Those involved may determine that the task is too hard and that they should "let someone else" reach that community. My point is that none of the motivations just mentioned are enough to keep a replanting pastor and his church excited, focused, and sacrificially committed to the goal over the long haul.

Worse yet, if a replanting pastor uses pragmatics to motivate the church to change, members will bail on him when the pain of change gets too high—and eventually, I promise, it will become too high. It always does. But if the church's goal is to make much of

Jesus—to bring him the glory he so richly deserves—and if that goal remains paramount throughout the process, everyone involved will have the courage to keep pushing forward.

Understanding and embracing the fact that replanting a church is an act of worship changes the motivation for replanting. We are doing this so that the glory of God is made known, so those who don't yet know God through the saving power of his Son, Jesus, can know him and glorify him. If replanting is an act of worship, then the struggle, the hardship, the pain, and the burden that comes with it, for the leader and the flock, have a real and powerful purpose. The purpose of the pain and the struggle is the glory of God. And when we remain focused on that truth, the pain becomes a joy.

Replanting churches is still not easy. As you read this book, you will quickly discover that replanting a dying church isn't for the faint of heart. If you are looking for a low-stress, easy way to spend the next five to ten years of your life, skip replanting a dying church. But if you are looking to spend the next decade of your life literally fighting for the glory of God, replanting a dying church may be for you.

CHAPTER 2

DIAGNOSING A DYING CHURCH

As you think about the struggling churches throughout North America, your mind will no doubt turn to a few specific congregations that are special to you. Maybe it's the church you attend or the church you pastor or a church that is special to someone else in your life. You are probably wondering, "Is this church just struggling through a 'phase' or is it in decline? Do we need to be patient or hit the reset button?" And, "If we do need to hit the reset button, do we do it here or do we start over somewhere else?" Those questions are important starting points. I hope this chapter helps as you think through the answers.

Characteristics of a *Dying* Church

In the past decade, I have had the privilege of working with many churches through the process of "repenting and remembering" that I mentioned in the previous chapter. I have noticed some common themes in churches that desperately need the invigoration of new life. Many of them show the following characteristics.

They value the process of decision more than the outcome of decision.

Dying churches love to discuss, debate, define, and describe. They live for business meetings—even if few people attend them. In the absence of meaningful ministry through the church, they often spend their time meeting together to make oftentimes meaningless decisions. Some of this can be attributed to the fact that they simply don't understand how to reach the community. They can't comprehend how to begin to make real and significant change, but they can still meet and go through the motions of the things they have done for decades. They begin to find comfort and security in the well-known processes of church life. It seems that as long as they continue the processes, they are keeping the church alive. It must also be said that sometimes their insistence on maintaining highly structured processes reflects a lack of trust in each other or certainly a lack of trust in leadership. They want to make sure no one "oversteps" his authority. The lack of trust and need for tight control is but another sign of a dysfunctional church.

They value their own preferences over the needs of the unreached.

Dying churches tend to make their preferences paramount. Those preferences can include music, programs, preaching styles, uses of the building, resources shared with those outside the church compared to resources used for those within the church, and a host of other things. The point is this: Most members of the congregation focus on their own desires in these decisions instead of what would meet the needs of people who don't know Jesus. They may passionately deny that they value their preferences over the needs of the lost, but here are a couple of tests.

Interview some unchurched people in the community. Ask them if: (a) they would prefer to sit in pews where they might have to crawl over someone who chose to sit on the aisle, or if they would prefer comfortable padded chairs with an appropriate "personal" space between them. Ask them: (b) if they would feel more at ease and comfortable if they were served coffee and allowed to drink it in the worship center. If the majority of the unchurched answered "yes" to A and B, how willing might the dying church be to pivot on a dime and make those changes? A church whose pursuit, with the heart of Christ, is the salvation of souls will thoughtfully and sacrificially consider the interests of others more valuable than the mere personal preferences of the establishment.

They have an inability to pass leadership to the next generation.

They may want young people in the congregation. They may complain endlessly about the lack of young people in the church, but they have no strategic plan in place to identify and place into positions of real and meaningful leadership young leaders, or worse yet, they tend to fight any attempt to put young people in charge of significant ministry efforts. If they do put a young person in a leadership position, the church micromanages him or criticizes him until he just leaves. Leaders will lead. If you don't provide young leaders the opportunity to lead in your church, they will eventually go somewhere else where they *can* lead. You can't attract and maintain young people if you don't afford them the chance to lead.

They cease, often gradually, to be part of the fabric of their community.

Members of dying churches rarely live within walking distance of the church. They have typically long ago moved to other parts of town. What was once a community church has become a commuter church. Members drive to the church building, park their cars, walk inside, and conduct their programs then walk back outside, get back in their cars, and drive home. It matters little to most members that the church is even in that neighborhood. Most significantly, the church pays little attention to the needs of the community, and the community pays little attention to the ebbs and flows of the church. If the church closed tomorrow, it is likely that no one in the neighborhood would fear losing their quality of life or that the neighborhood would be negatively affected.

They grow dependent upon programs or personalities for growth or stability.

Declining churches reach for programs and personalities they believe will turn the church around without embracing the changes needed to become healthy again. And it's hard to blame them for this predisposition since many past church-growth methodologies relied heavily on both. No doubt, as a dying church reflects on its heyday of growth, members recall a particular pastor or two who, by sheer force of personal charisma and leadership, moved the church to a new level. Or they recall a program or series of programs that once attracted all ages of people to become involved in the life of the church.

With that history in mind, dying churches often think that applying programs and hiring personalities will be easy fixes to their problems. They quickly discover that neither fixes anything. In fact, their desire for a "silver bullet" program or personality reinforces their belief that they don't have to make major changes or repent of past mistakes or sacrifice their preferences for the needs of the unchurched, but they just have to add one more program or hire one more professional to fix the problem. In essence, they are still trying to use primarily attractional methods in a community that no longer responds to those methods. It is frustrating and confusing for a dying church to accept that what worked so well in the past may, in fact, be hastening its demise.

They tend to blame the community for a lack of response and, in time, grow resentful of the community for not responding as it once did.

Declining churches are often slow to believe the problem lies within. Instead of embracing Jesus' call to transform their nearby community, they tend to believe they need protection from it. They may make attempts at community engagement. They may have a block party or give away food and clothing, but when no one attends Sunday school or morning worship as a result of these attempts, the church's resentments are reinforced. "They will take our food, jump in our bounce house, eat our cotton candy, and we never see them again" is a refrain I have heard many times.

Dying churches often mistakenly assume the community is there for them. They see the community as the resource from which they can grow, when in fact they need to understand that the truth is just the opposite. The community is not there for the church; the church is there for the community. We don't have block parties to get people from the community into our building; we have block parties to get the people in our building into the lives of the people in the community. The fact that the community doesn't respond is ultimately seen by the dying church as a problem with the community, rather than a problem with the church.

They anesthetize the pain of death with an overabundance of activity and maintaining less fruitful governance structure.

Church members who remember the church's heyday often feel intense disappointment over the current fruitlessness of the church. Instead of making the necessary changes to turn things around, they simply get busy doing "church stuff." Many believe that to quit these longtime practices of the church is to abandon the legacy of previous generations.

It is common for a church that is near death, with only a handful of remaining members, to continue to have a full slate of church activities. They continue with committee meetings and various programs that reach no one but maintain a sense of continuity with the past. There is also the sense that just being busy is a form of obedience. That in itself can become a source of pride. All of this activity—including maintaining a full church calendar, committee meetings, church meetings, and maybe even maintaining a church office and printing a newsletter—can distract a dying church from the fact that they are dying.

The structure of the church and its governance were likely designed when the church was much larger. Now, as the church is in decline, that structure is often a burden that prevents the church from making decisions in a timely manner and prohibits a quick pivot to join God where he is at work around them. They mistake maintaining the structure and particular governance style of the church with maintaining the church itself.

They confuse caring for the building with caring for the church and the community.

Often, declining churches see no difference between the building and the church. The primary motivation of the remaining members may be to "keep the church doors open" or to make sure they don't lose possession of the place that has meant so much to them throughout the years. At times, the most important and coveted committees in the congregation revolve around the church's properties and facilities. More and more of the time, attention, and resources of the church find their way into maintaining the building. It's not unusual for several meetings to be consumed with endless discussions about a roof, mechanical systems, or maintaining the lawn. While these issues may need attention, they seem to become the primary reason the church exists. To be frank, it is easier to spend time and money fixing a building than doing the hard work to become an indispensable part of the fabric of the community.

If you have spent any time around struggling churches, you have likely noticed many of these characteristics. It's tempting, when you do, to wonder, "Can this dying church be saved?" As you consider whether your church should be replanted, this is a critical truth to remember: *God can only replant a dying church if the people are willing to seek him, his glory, and his plan above all else.*

Should We Replant?

In reality, not every church should be saved. That may seem overly harsh and maybe even a completely new concept for you, but some churches should die. Jesus promises *The Church* will never die—and it won't. But local expressions of the church have come and gone since the days the New Testament was written. Think about the churches we read about in the Bible. You would be hard-pressed to find the same churches of Corinth, Ephesus, or Colossae that we read about in Paul's letters. They are gone today. New churches have been birthed in their place. The right question is never, "How can we save this church?" The right question is, "How can God get the most glory from our congregation right now?"

As mentioned before, I have worked with many churches that seemed to be near the end of their life. I have walked with them as they have tried to decide whether to replant the church, whether to let it die so remaining members can join other fellowships, or whether they should restart the congregation elsewhere. I have known and celebrated churches who have made each of those decisions. As churches struggle through this important process, I have them think through a few specific questions.

Is the church in a location where there is a need for a new church?

Sometimes churches die because the surrounding neighborhood has completely disappeared. Often, it's because what once was a residential area is now mostly full of industry and warehouses. Don't try to replant a church that no longer has a neighborhood around it. In a replanting situation in particular, your surrounding neighborhood is your primary mission field. If the church exists to serve the local community but you no longer have a local community, you may have no reason for a church. Move somewhere else.

As a corollary to this, determine if the neighborhood is already saturated with gospel-preaching and theologically solid churches. Just as a church planter assesses neighborhood need before planting, so should the replanter. See if any segment of the neighborhood isn't being reached by gospel-preaching churches. If there is no such segment, move on. There are plenty of places in North America in need of healthy churches. Go where there is a need.

Is the building usable and worth keeping? Is it cost-effective?

Never try to replant the church just to save a building. If the building is in such disrepair or has major environmental or structural issues that fixing it will lead you to spend more money than it's worth, don't do it. Remember, in dying churches, people will try to save the building at all costs. It gives them something to do. Don't let the emotional connection to a building decide whether you will invest kingdom resources where they shouldn't be invested.

Could the building be used as an incubator for multiple church plants or community ministry?

Replanted church buildings should be thriving places of ministry. The best buildings to use in replanting situations are those having the potential to be shared by other church plants or community ministries.

Many older churches have buildings far larger than they need, even if successfully replanted. Years ago, it wasn't at all unusual for a church to build a big building, perhaps 25 percent larger than their largest attendance. We have tens of thousands of neighborhood churches meeting in buildings far too large for their current context. Say, for example, you have a church that seats four hundred. You replant it, and it grows to one hundred. That's great! But to guests who attend your worship it doesn't so much appear there are one hundred people present as it appears there are three hundred people absent. The solution is to redeem the facility by inviting other church plants to share the space. Reclaim every inch of that building for the kingdom and strategically find ways to utilize it for kingdom purposes.

Your building communicates a message to your neighborhood. Dying churches often tell the neighborhood that the gospel is irrelevant and unimportant. But when people in a neighborhood see a building that once looked dead and now appears to be alive and filled with ministry and activity at all times during the day, they begin to see the church as an instrumental part of the neighborhood.

Helping a congregation make the all-important decision of whether to be replanted in the neighborhood or not is an emotional and difficult decision.

These questions must be gone through slowly and deliberately with objective observers whose advice you trust. It takes research. It takes much discussion—both inside and outside the church. Don't rush it. Pray as a church family through this decision. Ask others to pray with you. Consider an intense season of prayer, and consider including fasting as well. The glory of God in your neighborhood is, in one sense, at stake. Never forget that.

CHAPTER 3

REPLANTING PATHWAYS

God's glory must compel us to replant the dying churches that surround us in North America. The issue isn't pragmatics. We don't want to see churches replanted just because we don't want to see their resources wasted. (Although we don't want to see that either.) We don't want to see churches replanted just to make us feel better about the abysmal death rate among evangelical churches. We want to replant churches so God will be glorified as he does what he does best— bringing life out of death.

Dying churches have several characteristics in common. (See the list in chapter 2.) They are clearly at the end of their life cycles. In the denomination of the Southern Baptist Convention, with more than nine hundred SBC churches each year closing their doors, it is clear that there are at least forty-five hundred SBC churches that find themselves within five years of closing. But how those churches get to that point is different for each one. For example, their contextual situations are different. We find dying churches in rural areas where they are the only churches for miles upon miles, in sprawling suburbia, in the withering urban ring on the edges of major metro areas, in the thriving downtowns, and everywhere in between. Some are predominantly Anglo. Others are predominantly African-American. Others are non-English-speaking congregations. We also find a variety of stories as to why they are now in decline. For some, the arc of decline has been rapid with clear initiators, such as a church split or moral failure by the pastor. Others have seen their decline spread out over decades.

Do not make the assumption, however, that most of the dying churches are new church plants that don't make it or churches in remote, depopulating regions. A 2013 NAMB Research study of 903 churches that have ceased to exist revealed that 77 percent were in metropolitan communities (with population more than 50,000) and an additional 12 percent were in micropolitan communities (with population range of 10,000 to 50,000). Only 11 percent were in communities having fewer than ten thousand people. Eighty percent of churches that ceased to exist were more than five years old. We are closing churches where we need to plant churches.

The variety of declining churches in North America means there's no one-size-fits-all solution for replanting them. As I have met with replanting leaders throughout North America over the past few years, I have defined four different broad pathways churches can take in order to start fresh. Each carries its own challenges and opportunities.

Give the Building to a Church Plant

Of the four basic approaches to replanting churches and continuing the legacy of a church, this one may be the simplest. It works nearly every time it is tried. A dying church simply hands the keys to their building over to a church planter who will either start a brand-new church or another campus of a larger church that is committed to reaching that neighborhood using a multicampus approach.

Although this one may be the simplest of all approaches in replanting, it can also be the most difficult for the struggling church to accept. It isn't easy for a church that has a long history of ministry in a building to decide to simply hand it over to a new generation. I get that. But it is an incredibly important decision that we need to encourage more and more in the coming years in North America.

Each year in my denomination we plant more than one thousand new churches. God is calling men to plant churches. God is planting new churches by the thousands at just the time when thousands of existing churches with buildings are at the end of their life cycles. I pray that an ever-increasing number of dying churches will experience new life by letting go of the past and making their buildings available to a new church plant.

Like many of you, I have had the experience of walking with my parents through the aging process. There came a point in their life where they had to cede some of their independence to someone else. Though it's part of the aging process and happens to just about everyone, it's a tough conversation to have with your parents—*particularly your parents*. I know not everyone has this experience, but my parents were my heroes. I didn't want to discuss with them what they could no longer do, but those were incredibly important conversations. As we age, either we decide when we will make this transition, or the decision is made for us. And that's much tougher.

A similar dynamic comes into play when discussing with a once-thriving church how they might provide their building to a new generation of on-mission believers. But it is a critical conversation that we need to make more common. As I have mentioned in the previous chapters, we have nearly nine hundred churches in my own denomination (SBC) alone that cease to exist every year. Often, after a church ceases to exist, those buildings are lost to kingdom causes. That's tragic, particularly since thriving church plants and larger churches are looking for and sacrificing for buildings to use as ministry points.

But over the past few years, I have seen God do incredible work through the generosity of dying churches. As they have given their buildings to church plants or larger churches looking to add campuses, God has begun to bring new life to the surrounding neighborhoods.

Take what God did through a 174-year-old church in Greenwood, Missouri. Struggling for years, the church had been through several church splits and a damaging scandal when the leadership contacted Lenexa Baptist Church in Lenexa, Kansas, for help. Though the Greenwood church still had about one hundred people left, the church's rate of decline made it clear they needed to make a major change.

Because leadership transfer is such a critical issue when replanting a dying church, Lenexa Baptist made the terms clear up front. The church would need to relinquish all of its leadership of the ministry and all of its property to Lenexa Baptist. Lenexa Baptist would shut down the church and restart it under a different name. Lenexa Baptist also spent about $400,000 to upgrade the facilities, including renovating the sanctuary. A year after Lenexa Baptist took over the building, they called a lead pastor for the campus. The new lead pastor grew the church from about one hundred in attendance to about two hundred in the first year.

Steve Dighton, who was the senior pastor of Lenexa Baptist at the time says campuses like Greenwood where they have replanted struggling churches have been their most successful numerically. Two of Lenexa Baptist's five campuses were replanting situations. The church went through a similar process with a struggling church in Bonner Springs, Kansas, as well. That campus has tripled in size since the transition. Dighton believes that having a permanent meeting location and a core group to start with have helped the two replanted campuses grow at a faster rate than other campuses.

Share the Building with a Church Plant

Struggling churches can also choose to open their buildings to new church plants. Often we come across declining churches that aren't quite ready to make the drastic changes necessary to fully replant the church. They may still have a pastor who isn't ready to leave and who may not be the change agent the church needs. Likewise the church is not able to effectively reach its community. The church loves Jesus, and they love each other; however, the community has changed and, despite their efforts, they can't break its "missional code." These churches often find themselves with much more room than they actually need for the ministries of their church. Churches like this have the potential to extend their legacies for generations to come by becoming key partner churches for new church plants.

Finding a place for a new church to meet is one of the biggest hurdles church plants have to cross. For church plants that are just getting started, proper meeting spaces can be cost-prohibitive and tough to find. When a declining church opens its building to a new church plant (or maybe even multiple new church plants), it can play a critical role in helping the church plant make it through a key transition point. The new church plant can, in fact, provide a fresh look at the community. The new church can perhaps impact the neighborhood in a new and meaningful way. Oftentimes the new church can model for the older church a more missional and less attractional model of ministry that may be needed to reach the immediate community.

I saw this happen firsthand with Armour Heights Baptist Church in Kansas City. For years congregants had struggled to reach the community and had few results to show for their efforts. Their building was big enough to house several churches, so they decided to open it to a new church start. Armour Heights and the new church plant worked together on children's and youth ministries and Vacation Bible School. It didn't take long for Armour Heights to gain new vision and begin to grow themselves. The proximity—in location and ministry vision—to a new church plant had helped to build excitement at Armour Heights. I'm convinced it can do the same thing in many other churches throughout North America.

In fact, sometimes the shared excitement and ministry between the two will lead the two churches to merge. This happened with Community Baptist Church in Bellingham, Washington. Community Baptist had been in slow decline for years when it decided to open its church to a Spanish-language church plant. As the new church developed, the two churches ended up merging and forming one Spanish-language church. The new merged church ended up starting an English-language church soon afterward in the same building.

The truth is, an old building that seems too big for a declining church can be a blessing to a new church start and can help propel both churches forward in their Great Commission efforts. Declining churches don't need a large staff or a multimillion-dollar budget to be a partnering church for a new church plant. They simply need to practice the ancient Christian art of hospitality by sharing their building with churches that are just getting started.

Merge with a Church Plant

The first two options mentioned in this chapter are probably the simplest of the four approaches, though no replanting situation is easy, of course. They require the fewest changes from the struggling church. Give your building to a new church plant or to a larger church as a campus and you don't have to make any changes in how you do ministry. *Instead, you cease to exist as a church.* Some people in the congregation will choose to attend the new church, but they have no illusions regarding the continuity of the dying church's ministry. When a declining church hosts a new church plant in its building, it has to make few accommodations. Hopefully, the two begin to do joint ministry, but the declining church has no need to make wholesale changes in its ministry plans at the time it opens up its building.

That's not true with the last two options. For a church merger to work, the declining church will have to surrender much—if not all—of its ministry preferences. People will leave. It is inevitable—and usually healthy—in a church merger like this. It's not something that can be or should be attempted without much prayer and considerable courage on the part of the declining church and the new church plant.

The people of LifeConnection Church and Birchwood Baptist in Independence, Missouri, know this all too well. LifeConnection had been looking for a building to call home for some time when Birchwood Baptist, who was experiencing some decline, reached out to them about a possible merger. Birchwood had been mirroring a familiar narrative for some time. The aging congregation no longer fit the neighborhood's primary demographic. Closing wasn't imminent, but further decline seemed to be.

I had the privilege of walking with these two churches through this journey. Though it wasn't an easy process, the two prayed through the decision and voted in fall of 2014 to join forces. Birchwood Baptist provided the building.

LifeConnection Church provided the energetic leadership. LifeConnection Church's pastor, Jason Allen, realized from near the start that leadership couldn't rest in both churches. The new church needed a singular vision. So a big part of the merger journey rested upon Birchwood Baptist members learning to accept the vision and direction of LifeConnection Church. Some ministries had to end. Some traditions had to cease. A church that had years of faithful service to the community but had recently begun to decline was able to humble itself and accept the new leadership of a younger church. It wasn't easy, but it was beautiful to watch from my vantage point.

In the first three months following the two churches' merger, the new congregation averaged three hundred in attendance. What's so thrilling about that number is that it's more than the average attendance of both churches combined before the merger. The new church was far more than the sum of its parts. That's what you pray for before you start down this road. People are attracted to thriving churches that now sit where declining ones previously did.

Recently Pastor Allen shared with me that many of the older members from the former church are now fully on board in every way. When I asked why he thought that had happened, his answer was quick and to the point. Allen said the older members told him that they love these young leaders because, "they preach the Bible and they work hard."

In merging an old and a new church, the multiple generations can become a major source of blessing and strength to one another. In his book *Mergers*, Matt Rogers provides great insight and process for mergers.

Replanting from Within

The final replanting pathway may be the most familiar. It was the approach I took at Wornall Road. It also may be the most challenging and rewarding. Replanting from within means the declining congregation becomes a core group, of sorts, for a brand-new church. The replanting pastor has to do the work both of a pastor and a church planter. He will shepherd the longtime members of the church and warm their hearts to the gospel as he evangelizes and disciples a whole new group of people. At times he will feel as though he has two different congregations that he has to patiently move in the same direction, toward the same end.

As in the other three scenarios, churches looking to make this kind of change must be willing to change leadership. That's nonnegotiable. If you don't change the leadership, the church structure, the way decisions are made, and the church culture, the church will get the same results as it has been getting. The best-case scenario for this situation would be to make this transition when the former pastor has retired or moved to a new ministry.

It is also best if the church gives up day-to-day "command and control" to an outside partner. This can take many forms, but the bottom line must be a willingness to let go of the past and relinquish control. The degree to which they relinquish control, of every aspect of the church, is directly proportional to the probability of the success of the replant. The more control they insist on maintaining, the less likely the replant will succeed.

I am often asked what it takes for remaining members of a church to relinquish such control. Unfortunately the most common answer is, when they can no longer pay their utilities. It seems for many churches, as long as they have any ability to continue as they are, they delay the inevitable day when they must make significant change.

In sharing with these churches I have used the illustration of Moses's mother. She cared for him as long as she could and as best she knew how. But when she could no longer hide him herself, she built the basket and placed him in the river. She trusted the future of her son to the providential care of God. She let go. There comes a time in many dying churches when we acknowledge that the remaining members have done all they can do. Now we need to help them release this church to the care of him who is the Chief Shepherd. It must have been hard for Moses's mother to release her son to what was to her an unknown future. But her faith in God's sovereignty was greater than her fear. As I work with dying churches, I seek to bring them to this point of decision as they trust Jesus to care for his church and let go.

Though the other three scenarios will likely have much higher success rates than this one, I believe the vast majority of the declining churches that will be helped in the coming years will replant from within. I have noticed a marked increase in the number of churches that are seeking and accepting help before they run out of money.

My experience tells me that a few years ago most of the matriarchs and patriarchs of dying churches were members of the "greatest generation." This amazing generation endured the Great Depression and fought World War II. They didn't quit. The thought of giving up or walking away from responsibility was unthinkable. This was true in their church life as well. They would never give up and were reluctant to let go. While this had been their greatest strength throughout their lives, it could become a detriment in regard to leading a declining church.

That generation is nearly gone. I am finding that the matriarchs and patriarchs of many of today's dying churches are aging baby boomers. Let's just say many of them are more likely to turn over leadership and step aside. On the whole they may not want to spend all their retirement years simply keeping a church building open. I am convinced this gives us a great opportunity for replanting in the decade to come.

To replant all these churches, we will need a new generation of called, gifted young men. Not every pastor and not every church planter is called to serve as a replanter. (See chapter 7 for a full explanation of the unique qualities needed to be a replanting pastor.)

Bob Bickford is one of those uniquely called and uniquely equipped replanting pastors we need to develop more of in the years to come. Bickford arrived at Sherwood Baptist Church in Webster Grove, Missouri, in 2012 to serve as its lead pastor. Started in 1958, the church connected well with its community for about a decade, peaking in 1967 with two hundred fifty people. Nearly five decades of decline followed as the church looked less and less like the community that surrounded it. Bickford says the church members wanted their church to grow again, but they really didn't know how to make that happen.

When Bickford arrived at Sherwood, he led the church to make some expected changes. The church modernized its music, streamlined the church schedule, and updated the church facilities. But he also did the hard work of a church planter. He spent significant time in the community, building relationships with new people, sharing the gospel, and discipling new people. He led the church to serve the community with radical abandon. Most important, Bickford majored on the gospel. He warmed the hearts of the church toward the good news about Jesus.

Bickford said, "The first thing we had to do is help the church fall in love with Jesus again, to understand the gospel and what it means in our lives."

The church, which has been renamed The Groves, now averages around sixty adults and twenty kids in attendance. Most important, the church is growing and is relevant again to its community.

With more than nine hundred churches in my own denomination that cease to exist each and every year, all of these options should be on the table as we look for ways to bring new life to struggling churches. Each of these options has strengths and weaknesses. But I'm convinced that as struggling churches look to extend their legacies to the next generation, each of these four options—and maybe even some fresh options I haven't listed here—must be taken seriously.

CHAPTER 4

SIX REPLANTING IMPERATIVES

As discussed in the previous chapter, no two declining churches are the same. Each has its own story, its own reasons for decline. I'm convinced that God has a unique path of rebirth for each of them. Still, as I have connected with replanting pastors around the country, I have noticed six specific practices that were part of just about every replanting process. I call them replanting imperatives because they are critical to the success of the replanting effort.

However, replanting churches aren't alone in needing to demonstrate these imperatives. In many ways they should be part of every healthy church that reflects its community. But for replanting churches, they are even more critical. Why? You have no room for error when you replant a declining church. It's tough enough when these six components are present. It's nearly impossible when they are not.

There is no order to these imperatives. You need all six throughout the entire process. You will never outgrow or move beyond any of them. You don't need to get down the first one and move on to the next one. You need to work at all of them, all the time. While they are particularly important for the replanting pastor, it is critical that everyone be on the same page about them. What are the six imperatives?

Pray without Ceasing

Above everything else, the work of replanting a church is a spiritual process—and it's a battle. Satan does not like the work of replanting a dying church. He wants the church to die. He wants your neighbors to look at the church and see it as an impotent, dying fossil of another era. He will do whatever it takes to stop what God wants to do in a declining church. Unfortunately, in looking at how many churches die each year, it appears Satan frequently succeeds in this effort.

That is why it would be foolish and arrogant to attempt the work of replanting a church without an effective prayer strategy. We wouldn't dare send a church planter into a new community without making sure he understands the power and necessity of prayer, including how to mobilize others to pray for him. It wouldn't be optional. It wouldn't be novel. It would be how the work would get done. Yet too many replanting pastors attempt to do similar work without the needed prayer support.

Remember the story of Jesus crossing the Sea of Galilee and meeting a demon-possessed man? Before the demons were cast out of the man, they begged Jesus not to send them out of the country. I am not sure why they asked Jesus that, but I have often wondered if it was for this reason: Satan will never easily give up dominion over that which he has gained. Satan won't want to leave just because you show up. Satan has been robbing God of his glory in that church for years, and he won't give up that territory without a fight.

If you don't cry out to God in consistent, passionate prayer, you won't replant a church. You also need to engage others to covenant with you in prayer. John Piper says, "Prayer is wartime communication." If you were pinned down on Omaha Beach as the Allies were invading on D-Day and you were fortunate enough for someone to throw you a radio, you would call your fellow soldiers on one of the allied ships and tell them where to aim the shells to take out the artillery that is bearing down on you. That's what it's like for us as we replant churches. We have to spend time in prayer, pleading with God to take down the strongholds in our churches and in our communities. Without prayer we are powerless to replant.

Love the Church's Remaining Members

When you replant a dying church, you can't forget that you are called to be the church's pastor. In fact, you are called to be *the whole church's pastor,* not just the young, hip people who have joined the church since your arrival. That means you have to love the older members of the church who have been there for years. Even when they are not happy with some of the changes you are leading the church to make, you still love them. You learn about their interests. You remember their birthdays and their anniversaries. You must visit and care for widows. You listen to their stories, particularly their stories of the church when it was thriving. You never get so busy trying to turn the church around that you forget your calling as a pastor. If you can't love a multigenerational church, forget about being a replanting pastor. You will do more disservice than service to the kingdom.

You also don't blame the older members for the church's struggles. They are not the reason the church isn't thriving. The truth is someone, a former pastor or many former pastors, failed these people. They are the kind of church members they are because of the men who have led them. They may be contrary. They may criticize and condemn. They may gossip and plot against you. But they do that because previous pastors and leaders failed to model church leadership for them. They were never disciplined for such behavior. In fact, if they "ran off" a pastor, they felt—in effect— rewarded for that behavior. It reinforced that this behavior is a way to achieve their goals.

The bottom line is that you have a lot of pastoral care to do with these folks. It isn't going to happen quickly, but don't give up on them. They are the ones Jesus has entrusted to you. This is one of the differences between a replant and a plant. In a plant, you essentially choose with whom you start. In a replant you start with those who are already there. You also don't expect the remaining members to be the change agents and to lead the church to where it's going to be in the future. You just love them. You let them know how much they mean to you and how much they mean to God.

In the process, you warm their hearts to the gospel. Remind them of what the gospel is over and over again. Preach it. Teach it. Model it. Remember though, this isn't primarily a head issue. Most of your older members have been reciting the gospel for decades. They know it. Your job is to help them rediscover it with their hearts. Remind them of how desperate their need is for Jesus. Ask them to share their stories of coming to Christ and to recount times in their lives when God was very real to them.

Take every sermon and every conversation and look for ways to help them see that their true joy comes in what Jesus has done for them and not in what they can do for the church or what the church can do for them. Help them see that true joy will come as they experience the gospel and pass it on to future generations. That must be a constant theme of your communication. As you spend time with them, enjoying their company and helping them rediscover this message, you will watch their hearts warm to the gospel.

You will never be able to guilt the longtime members of the church into making sacrifices for the sake of the gospel. If you find yourself tempted to go down that road, stop it. Guilt is an awful motivator for ministry. In fact, many of them have been "guilted" into serving their entire Christian lives. This has created many unhappy legalists. Telling the elderly saints of the church that if they don't change the church will die may (and even this is doubtful) change their behavior in the short-term, but it will never warm their hearts toward the gospel and make long-term changes in their lives and the life of the church. They must realize that by making much of Jesus and sharing his story they will find true joy.

The writer of Ecclesiastes 12 admonishes readers to "remember your Creator in the days of your youth: Before the days of adversity come . . ." (v. 1). He goes on to describe the pain, fear, and dread of old age. Let's be clear. It's no fun getting old. Family moves away, loved ones die, careers come to an end, technology changes too quickly for many to adapt. As the writer of Ecclesiastes truthfully describes, these are "evil days" (12:1 ESV).

But compare the passage in Ecclesiastes to Paul's beautiful passage from Philippians 4:11–13: "I don't say this out of need, for I have learned to be content in whatever circumstances I am. I know both how to have a little, and I know how to have a lot. In any and all circumstances I have learned the secret of being content—whether well fed or hungry, whether in abundance or in need. I am able to do all things through Him who strengthens me."

There it is! The key to joy in old age! It is not holding onto the past. It is not maintaining the familiar. It is not singing the same songs and doing church the same way. The key to joy in the "evil days" of old age is Jesus. As we replant, we must with great passion for God's glory and our members' joy lead them to lay down the idol of nostalgia for the past (which never satisfies), and to embrace that which can bring joy without end in every season of life—Jesus, our beautiful Redeemer.

Many have said the only catalyst for change is pain. While that is true in the human sense, I don't want to lead a church where people have changed only to avoid pain. The real catalyst for lasting and transforming change is to lead them to embrace a greater joy and more precious treasure than nostalgia and control.

At Wornall Road, one way I warmed the hearts of the older members was through hymns. When I arrived at the church, longtime members made it clear to me how important the old gospel hymns were to them. So we kept singing them, but we didn't stop with just singing them. I preached the hymns to them.

I reminded them *why* they loved those hymns and what the words of those hymns really meant. Since many of those hymns were deeply immersed in the gospel, it was a great way to teach the gospel in a way that made the church's longtime members eager to listen.

I also began preaching exegetical sermons. No more "Bible Bingo" of one passage and topic one week and another the next. No, we began and continue to have a systematic "through the book" approach to preaching. And in the preaching we emphasize the thread of the gospel and the cross that is woven throughout Scripture. As W. A. Criswell used to say, we preach the "scarlet thread of redemption" from Genesis to Revelation, and Spurgeon encouraged his students to "preach the cross" in every sermon. For many of these remaining members it has been a long time since they were exposed to this kind of focused, gospel-saturated preaching. If they truly are converted, their hearts will in time respond to this type of preaching.

I met Forrest Lowe on my first Sunday at Wornall Road. A World War II veteran and an engineer by trade, Forrest was a man who usually told things just as they were with very little fluff. Wornall had a long, distinguished history with music in the church's heyday. Many, including Forrest, were not happy with recent pastors trying to transition to other styles of music. When I first came to the church and asked Forrest what was going on at the church, he told me, "Walk in this church now and it's like a Branson country music show on that stage. If I want Branson country music shows I go to Branson, not church." That was Forrest and what mattered to him at that point in the life of the church.

Over the next few months and years I spent a lot of time around Forrest. I started learning what made him tick. I watched as he cared for an ailing wife who was not physically able to come to church or anywhere else anymore. I spent time enjoying his hobbies with him. I asked him questions and encouraged him to share his stories. Though he was years older than I was, I discipled him like I might disciple a man my junior. As time went by, God changed him in incredible ways, and the changes he enabled at Wornall came to benefit him in tangible ways. When his dear wife passed away, six young men, our key leaders at Wornall, were privileged to serve as her pallbearers. None of the six were at Wornall when the replant began. They all loved Forrest. I can tell you one thing for sure about Forrest today: he cares more about the gospel and passing it to the next generation than he does about Wornall's style of music.

Exegete the Community

As a replanter, you must do the work of a church planter. You have to get to know your neighborhood. If you can't reach the neighborhood surrounding your church, you can't replant the church. It's really that simple. Even if the neighborhood has changed drastically around the church, you must reach what is there today.

That won't be easy at first. More than likely, one of the reasons the church has been declining is because its demographics no longer match the demographics of the neighborhood. Often, most of the remaining congregants of the church do not live within walking distance of the church. Yet it is the local neighborhood around your church that must be your priority. If there is no longer a surrounding neighborhood and the church is now in the middle of industry rather than residences, you likely don't want to replant the church there. Sell the building, and look elsewhere to start a new church.

As you exegete (assess) your community, you will look to meet the unique spiritual and physical needs of your neighbors. Exegeting a community is far more than downloading demographics. You need to immerse yourself in the community. Attend community meetings. Volunteer to serve in the community in any way you can. Shop regularly in the community. Get your hair cut by the same barber at the same time each month. Talk to the men in the barbershop. Same goes for coffee shops, dry cleaners, cafés, and grocery stores. Get to know the names of the people who work in these places. Learn their stories and let them tell you stories of the community. Volunteer at the schools. Volunteer to coach youth sports. Maybe even join a softball team or bowling league. Become an expert on your community. If there is a bus stop nearby, consider showing up in the mornings to ride the bus as people are going to work. Get to know the people at the bus stop. Bring them coffee on a cold morning. Volunteer to ride along with the police in your community.

Serve your community with abandon as you work to meet the specific needs you have discovered. Do this from the first day you begin replanting the church. Don't wait until you have leaders to do this. If you don't have people to help, access your denominational network. At Wornall Road, we took advantage of the huge amount of human resources available to us as Southern Baptists. Through our local association, state convention, and the North American Mission Board, we were able to bring in people to help us meet needs until we developed leaders who could participate.

For a normative-sized church of around one hundred fifty, Wornall Road has made an enormous ministry footprint in our neighborhood. In just the past four years, we have been featured on local television news at least twenty-five times—and all of them in a positive manner. As we have looked to meet the needs of the neighborhoods and serve people with the love of Jesus, people have taken notice. You don't redefine your church for your community by changing your name, updating your sanctuary, or changing your music. You redefine the church for your community by how you serve it. You don't serve your community to get people into your church either. You serve the community to get your church, the people of your church, into the lives of the people in the community on a consistent basis.

A few years back a top-notch student athlete in our community was killed in a random shooting. He had been a straight-A student without even a parking ticket on his record. I became very involved with the student's family, helping with a memorial service at the school. Through that experience, I discovered there was an epidemic of murders in our city, particularly in a neighborhood adjacent to ours. That year alone more than 115 people had been murdered in our city.

That October, and every October since, we put up a cross on our church lawn for every murder victim in our city. Each cross has the name of one of the victims on it and the date of his or her death. On December 20, we hold a Longest Night service at the church where we honor the memories of those victims. We invite their families, weep with them, share the gospel with them, and pray with them. At the end of the service, we all go outside and our members stand by each cross and embrace each family.

That's the only kind of Christmas service we have each year. Our community gets enough Christmas pageants. Our community needs people to weep with them and to reveal to them the power of the gospel in the midst of life's deepest pain. The county prosecutor's office works with us and local crime victims' groups and helps us invite every family who has lost a loved one to murder. It is still one of the most important ways Wornall Road serves its neighbors.

Simplify Your Strategy

A declining church of fewer than fifty people doesn't need the same structure and ministries it had when it ran one hundred fifty to two hundred. A replanted church must become a focused church. That refocused, simplified church looks different in every context. You will need to determine what your church's priorities look like as you strive to make disciples in your context.

Simplifying your church structure will have multiple benefits throughout the replanting process, but maybe the most important benefit is to give young families the needed margin to *live the Christian life*. That's how ministry is done these days. Older generations expected to be busy at church. Younger families do not. They need space to live their faith outside of the church building. Simplifying your strategy and reducing the time members are expected to be in the church building gives them that space.

At Wornall Road, we asked people to participate in three ways: weekly, gospel-centered worship; weekly community groups; and a lifestyle built around serving. We didn't expect people to do anything else. In fact, the only gathering at the church most weeks was the church worship service on Sundays. That gave our young families time to be involved in the community and to serve. Thom Rainer's book *Simple Church* is an excellent resource to help you think through this process with your church family.

Many older, dying churches have complex and detailed organizational structures that make the decision-making process slow and unresponsive. Your church structure needs to facilitate kingdom growth, not prohibit it. Many churches experienced failures or conflict in the past and, in an effort to see that "that never happens again," they put governance mechanisms in place to safeguard against missteps. Though perhaps well-intentioned, the result is often a governance system that slows down and deters missions/ministry activity rather than encouraging it. New churches can react quickly. They can saddle up in a hurry and move to the sound of the battle while dying churches argue over which saddles to use. You get the picture. Create a biblical model of church leadership that actually allows those selected to lead, to lead.

Focus on Reaching Young Men

One trait you will find in many declining churches is a failure to pass leadership on to the next generation. Declining churches may really love young people. They may swarm them when they come into the church and offer them food, help with the kids, and many kind words. The question isn't whether or not your church loves young people. The question is: Can your church pass leadership on to them? Can it hand over the keys to the church and then enjoy the ride? Leaders must lead. If you don't let young leaders lead, they will leave your church.

The desperate need for young leaders in a replanting situation is one of the reasons I believe you have to focus on reaching young men. I have never heard a dying church say, "We just have too many young men, we need to go out and attract some older people." I have also never seen a healthy church that is without a solid core of young men. Young male leaders are an indispensable part of replanting a declining church. If you can't reach and disciple one young man, you can't replant a church. Did you get that? *If you can't reach and disciple one young man, you can't replant.*

I would go so far as to say if you can't reach and disciple one young man, you should consider whether you are called to pastor at all. I would suggest that if you are unable to disciple even one young man it may be because you have never experienced being a disciple yourself. Unfortunately, there were times when men responded to God's call to ministry and were sent to Bible college or seminary without ever having been discipled. As a result, they have little success in creating disciples. If you are one of those men, please find someone to engage you in discipleship. Be discipled so you can disciple others.

You have limited time as a replanting pastor. You may have a full-time secular job to go along with your pastoral duties. You likely have a family to shepherd. You can't do everything. But one of the nonnegotiable parts of replanting a church is to focus like a laser on young men between the ages of eighteen and thirty-five. This doesn't mean you won't share the gospel with children or seniors or women. Of course, you will do that. But your time as a replanting pastor has to be focused on young men. For a dying church, gaining young male leaders is the game changer.

My guess is that if you look at the leadership of the church you are replanting during its peak years for reaching the neighborhood, you will find mostly men between the ages of eighteen and thirty-five (except maybe the pastor). For most of the history of the church, *young* men have made the biggest leadership impact on the mission of God. Think about Jesus' early disciples. We tend to think of Peter, John, James, and the rest of the Twelve as middle-aged people, but they weren't. Some suggest the majority of the disciples may have been teenagers. This suggestion is based on the story recorded in Matthew 17:24–27 where the coin in the fish's mouth was enough to pay the temple tax for Jesus and Peter and not for the rest of the disciples. At that time only men over the age of twenty were required to pay the tax. Teenagers or not, they certainly were not the aged-looking men we see in stained glass windows and famous religious paintings. Even Jesus was thirty-three years old when he went to the cross. Throughout the history of the world, God has often chosen to use young men to change the world. Why can't the same thing happen in your neighborhood through your church? It has often been said that most movements of God throughout history didn't begin with men my age (older than fifty), but men my age can quench those movements.

You want to invest in any relationship you have with young men, but you want to particularly focus on young, male leaders. You reach one young leader, and he will bring in more young men. It may take you three to four years to reach and mentor your first young man (especially if you are in a bivocational situation as I was in my first years at Wornall Road), but keep trying. Get involved in activities where young men are likely to be found. Hang out at the coffee shops. Volunteer to coach youth sports (where you will likely run into young dads). Go to the basketball courts where young men are playing. Part of your community exegesis must be to discover where young men are in your community and how you can be part of those gatherings.

It may be that what you are doing in mentoring young men won't happen in the context of the church for a while. Young men—particularly non-Christian young men—won't be interested in your work of replanting a church. For a time you may be loving on and caring for older members, working through leadership issues at the church, and connecting with young men in a completely different venue—maybe through one-on-one Bible study. It is through your church's community service that you will bring the two groups together. Young leaders—saved or not— who may not be interested in the life of your church will be interested in the work of your church if you are active and serving the community. As they see you and your church demonstrating your commitment to community improvement, they will want to be part of what's going on.

Make Disciples Who Make Disciples

Jesus gives his church clear instructions in Matthew 28:19–20:

"Go, therefore, and make disciples of all nations, baptizing them in the name of the Father and of

the Son and of the Holy Spirit, teaching them
to observe everything I have commanded you."

Nearly every evangelical church you go into will
recognize the Great Commission's call to make disciples as a core part of the church's mission. Yet most
of our churches struggle to do it. For the replanting
church, discipleship is theologically and pragmatically
essential. The replanting church needs to lead new
people to Christ, help them grow in their faith, and to
eventually reproduce themselves.

Growing up, discipleship for me was filling in a
discipleship notebook. I would learn Scripture, answer
questions, and measure my progress, primarily by how
much of the notebook I filled in. While away at camp,
I would get pretty good at filling it out every day during my devotional time. Then I would get back home
and for the first few days, or even weeks, I would continue my habit. Not only was this not discipleship, it
leaned, for me anyway, toward legalism. When I filled
out my notebook and kept my daily "quiet time," I
tended to be proud of my accomplishment. I would
be eager to go to youth group on Wednesday night so
I could share at the appropriate time just how "faithful" I had been. While I am confessing, I'll go ahead
and say it: I liked to compare myself to the "spiritual
slackers" of the group who missed a few days in their

quiet time that week. Yes, I was filled with pride, and that was a sin.

Then, invariably something would come up and I would miss a day or two along the way. Then I would feel so guilty that I didn't want to go to church because I didn't want to report my lack of discipleship activity. I didn't even want to start my quiet time again because I was embarrassed to come before God again and admit I hadn't been committed enough to get out of bed a few minutes early each day. So my "discipleship" led me to swing between pride and defeat, neither of which is joyful or Christ-honoring. Simply completing a notebook or a study course might have provided useful information, but it was in no way making me a disciple.

Discipleship isn't something you learn in a class or at a conference. Discipleship happens as you become who you hang out with. When we get concerned because our kids are struggling and hanging out with "the wrong kind of people," we are really concerned— and rightfully so—because those people are discipling our kids.

If you want your church to become a congregation that *makes disciples that make disciples,* you have to *get your people into discipling relationships with one another.* That has to be a foremost priority of your church. You must encourage engagement in discipleship in your preaching, teaching, and your conversations. You must model discipling others and being a disciple as well. You must create environments where relationships happen that form the basis for discipleship.

As I mentioned earlier, at Wornall Road we focus on strongly encouraging our members to be part of weekly worship, weekly community groups, and a lifestyle of service. Part of the reason it's so important to streamline your structure is so you leave room for what is truly important. Connecting your members in some kind of discipleship activity is one of those truly important elements you can't live without.

In fact, there's a reason I talk about this imperative last. *This is your scorecard.* (See chapter 6 for more about this.) Want to know if the replanting process has "worked" in your church? It is not when you reach a certain number in attendance or whether the church can afford to pay a pastor or whether people in the neighborhood now think of you as the "cool" church. You have succeeded if you are making disciples who make disciples who transform your community. Biblical discipleship never ends with the one being discipled. You are always discipling so that person disciples another, then another, then another. Do that and your neighborhood will be transformed. Businesses will be impacted. Schools will be impacted. Families will be impacted. And if your community is better because your church is there, you have succeeded. You have made it. And that's something to celebrate.

Remember, none of these imperatives are done sequentially or in isolation of the others. They are all done simultaneously, though of course they may be done at differing speeds depending upon your context. They also don't represent every significant decision a replanting church needs to make, but they do represent the primary ones. These six imperatives need to be firmly embedded in your preaching, teaching, conversations, and lifestyle. *The foundation for all of these imperatives is preaching that is Christ-centered, gospel-saturated, and grounded in the fidelity of the Scriptures.*

I believe these six imperatives represent important areas of focus for a church that wants to take the important step of reclaiming the glory of God in its neighborhood.

CHAPTER 5

STORIES OF TRANSFORMATION

As I have traveled throughout North America trying to help churches get a vision for replanting, it has become obvious that God is laying the groundwork for a new movement. I didn't describe the imperatives from the last chapter just because they worked in my context at Wornall Road. Not only have I seen them bear fruit in my context, but I have seen God use them in a variety of contexts in North America. You don't have to just take my word for how significant these imperatives are to a replanted church. Take the perspective of other leaders—born from their own pain and struggle—who have successfully replanted churches in their contexts.

The following stories illustrate the six replanting imperatives. I hope they will give you wisdom for your journey and a renewed hope that the God who sent his Son to die for the church longs to resurrect declining congregations throughout North America and the world. As you read these stories, ask yourself: Could God do this in my context?

Be prepared to hear him answer, *YES!*

Pray without Ceasing: Pleasant Ridge Baptist Church's Story

When Malachi O'Brien first visited Pleasant Ridge Baptist Church in Harrisonville, Missouri, he didn't expect it to be a regular trip. O'Brien, a student at nearby Midwestern Baptist Theological Seminary, was helping the church fill the pulpit while they looked for a new pastor. When the congregation asked him to consider becoming the church's new pastor, he thought the small, country church was the last place he would put down roots.

Pleasant Ridge had been anything but pleasant for pastors in its history. It had a reputation. In 148 years, forty-seven men had served as the church's pastor.

In the past twenty-five years alone, the church had split three times. But as the church began to talk with O'Brien and his family about the open pastoral position, God began to move his heart toward taking the position.

That's when God reminded O'Brien of a quote he had once heard: "God does his greatest of works in the hardest of places so he gets all the glory." When the church voted him in as its pastor in 2011, it was by a 29–2 vote. That vote included most of the regular Sunday worship attendance—including a few extras.

O'Brien could have started his work at Pleasant Ridge in many different directions. There were needs everywhere. Instead he started through prayer—an all-night prayer meeting within the first month he was pastor.

"I knew that the power of prayer and revival was our greatest need and our only hope," O'Brien said. "So when we went in there, the only thing I knew to do was to pray."

O'Brien invited a few friends who didn't attend the church to join him. Although he invited the entire church to participate in the all-night prayer effort, only one person from Pleasant Ridge showed up. Still, from 10:00 p.m. to 6:00 a.m., the handful of people prayed for every pew and every classroom in the church.

During the second month O'Brien held a late-night prayer gathering, from 8:00 p.m. to midnight, called "Fire in the Altars," that became a regular habit for the church. O'Brien also began mobilizing church leaders to pray on a regular basis for revival in the church.

The Lord began to do what only he can do. God drew families to the church who didn't seem to have any conceivable connection with the congregation—a miraculous feat considering how far out in the country the church is located.

"I was basically selling them dreams and visions at the time," O'Brien said. "Because we didn't have anything. We told them, 'If you stick around, we'll have awesome worship and awesome activities for your kids,' and they did stick around."

Through prayer, God began to tear down walls that only he could tear down. One watershed moment for Pleasant Ridge stood out. About seven months into O'Brien's time as pastor, he broke down in the pulpit, telling the congregation, "Church, I don't care about the numbers. I don't care if we're the largest church in the area or if anyone ever knows who we are. I just want to be a church where the presence of God dwells." The invitation went on for more than forty minutes, as people prayed at the altar and asked for God to send revival to the small, country church.

As the church stood on the doorsteps of revival, the attack from the enemy heated up as well. Longtime members, led more by fear than faith, found themselves losing control of the church. O'Brien said one longtime member told the young pastor one day that no one liked him and a group was going to meet later in the week to decide how to proceed. The group decided not to proceed with removing him. When the local newspaper wrote a compelling article about all God had done in the small church in a short time, one longtime member wrote a letter to the editor complaining that O'Brien was taking the church away from them.

But O'Brien continued to pray, and God continued to work. In the past four years the church has baptized seventy to eighty people. In the two years before O'Brien took the leadership of the church, six people were baptized. In the five years before that, no one was baptized.

"All we knew to do was pray, pray, pray, fast, and pray," O'Brien said. "So that's what we did."

Structural changes began to come as old barriers came down. Monthly business meetings went away. The church changed the worship style to match the people in the community. The name changed from Pleasant Ridge Baptist Church to The Church at

Pleasant Ridge. The youth ministry grew from two teenagers to more than forty on Wednesday nights.

"These teenagers aren't coming for fun. They are coming to get preached to. They're getting saved," O'Brien said. "Now the students are our prayer warriors. They're the ones coming to our late-night prayer gatherings. They're the ones meeting before church to pray in my office. There's not a Sunday that goes by that there aren't ten to fifteen teenagers at the altar praying."

O'Brien insists that desperate, passionate prayer is the heart of revitalizing and replanting churches like Pleasant Ridge Baptist Church. When God's people give themselves to prayer, God does what only he can do—revive the dying.

"I love the story of Ezekiel 37," O'Brien said. "Dry bones can live again and become a mighty army. I've seen it firsthand."

Love the Church's Older Members: Liberty Baptist Church's Story

As Dr. Tony Preston looked out at the congregation of Liberty Baptist Church in Liberty, Missouri, four years ago, he saw a church in decline. Baptisms were down. Attendance was down. While the population outside the church was getting younger, with the population between ages twenty-five and fifty-four growing most rapidly, the age trajectory of the church was headed in the other direction. Most were older than fifty-five.

"You're going to have to change or die," Preston, the interim pastor and associational director of missions, told the church. Though Preston's words may have been harsh, they were true, and the church knew it. Even today, many still remember those words as a "line in the sand" for the congregation.

In 2012 the church called Nathan Rose to be its next pastor. Rose had a luxury many replanters don't have. Though struggling and certainly headed for death in the future if changes weren't made, Liberty Baptist had time. Rose could be patient.

During the first year he made only a few changes. As Rose tells the story, he focused only on "low-hanging fruit," changes that would involve little conflict. Instead, the new pastor put his effort toward simply listening to church members and discovering appropriate ways to make changes within the congregation.

Toward the end of the first year, Liberty Baptist made two moves that set the stage for later church shifts. First, Rose said, the church began taking membership much more seriously. Previously, new members could walk the aisle at the end of the service and join the church on the spot. Rose started a membership class and began requiring new members to have an interview with him before joining the church so he could determine whether they had made a personal commitment to Christ previously. Liberty Baptist began contacting inactive members and taking them off the church rolls if they had died, moved, or showed little interest in returning.

At around the same time, Rose gathered a team from both new members (those who had joined the church in the year since Rose had arrived) and established, longtime leaders of the congregation. Over the next eight months, the group read through Thom Rainer's book *Simple Church* and looked honestly at where the church was heading and where the community was heading. Then they began to hammer out a plan for moving the church from where it was to where it needed to be. That meant taking a long, hard look at the discipleship process and what it meant to be a member at Liberty. After the eight-month process, the congregation as a whole passed the church's updated ministry plan.

Rose could have done what many other pastors looking to make significant changes in the church do and stopped right there. But he knew that making changes "like a bull in a China shop" wasn't the answer. That kind of change-making wouldn't be healthy for the church or him, Rose surmised.

"I don't believe you can make changes until you've made a proper assessment. I'm not the church's savior. The church had been around for forty-nine years at that time. They had done something right," Rose said. "Honestly, I didn't want to be 'that guy'—the one who comes in and thinks he knows everything. I simply didn't believe that."

Instead, Rose embraced his role as pastor to the whole church and, particularly, the longtime members who had invested much in the church's history. He listened and loved the members of the church. He spent time discovering where people were spiritually and personally. They needed a pastor at the time, Rose said, "who loved them where they were but wouldn't let them stay there."

Some days, as the church continued to transition, weren't easy. Rose remembered one particular time when a disgruntled longtime member looked like he wanted to take a swing at him. But Rose sat and listened even when it was difficult, taking seriously the perspective of the longtime members. When criticism came, Rose added, he just listened, trying as hard as possible to keep his mouth shut as he did. He realized responding defensively would only exacerbate the situation.

Rose also made a point to remember birthdays and anniversaries of church members. Each week he makes a list of upcoming special days. He then prays for and calls each of those who are celebrating those days. He does the same thing for widows in the congregation, remembering to pray for and call them or write a card to them on their birthdays and wedding anniversaries. He believes this practice has particularly blessed the more established members of the church.

Another important act of care for older members of the church has been visiting shut-ins and those who are sick. He takes his kids along as he does so, something older members appreciate. Plus, he makes it a point to serve together with the longtime members. For example, the older members visit the nursing home monthly, and Rose and his family join them.

Rose also encourages some of the new members to develop relationships with the older members. He particularly encourages younger members to use the church directory to learn the names of the older members. Recently, Liberty's younger members threw a Valentine's Day banquet for the older members, including a nice dinner and a photographer to provide mementoes for attendees.

"We've tried to celebrate and honor the past," Rose said. "We've been really careful not to communicate that the longtime members haven't been obedient to do what God has called them to do."

As Rose loved and cared for the congregation, both old and young alike, he also has made the gospel paramount. He based his first sermon at the church on 1 Corinthians 15:1–3 and literally preached the gospel. In the process he told the church, "Just so you know, everything we do is built upon and seen through a gospel lens. The gospel isn't just the message that saves us—although it is that—but it's the message that trans-forms us," Rose told the church in that first message.

As he shared that with the congregation, Rose set the stage for what would become the church's disciple-ship strategy. Ask the church's members why Liberty exists and they will tell you, "to be and to make dis-ciples." Ask them how Liberty does it and they will say, "by living in light of the gospel in worship, com-munity, and mission."

"The three things we do together as disciples of Jesus is we worship together, live in community together, and do mission together, but we don't do those things just because that's what good Christian boys and girls do," Rose said. "We do it as a response to the gospel."

Every message Rose preaches, he said, includes the gospel—not just as an add-on that tells people how to get saved—but as the means to real and meaningful transformation. The gospel unifies the church—both young and old, rich and poor, new to the faith or long-serving saints—under the banner of Jesus' redemptive work.

Rose said, "Do we come together and love one another just because that's what good, civilized people do? No. It's because as John tells us in 1 John 3:16, 'He laid down his life for us so we ought to do the same thing for our brothers.'"

Rose will be the first to tell you that God hasn't grown the church into a megachurch over the past three years, but he is thrilled with what the Lord has done. The demographics have changed dramatically in that the church is looking more and more like the community around it. Attendance is up. Finances have improved. Even Cooperative Program giving is up.

Rose is grateful that Liberty Baptist made the all-important decision to change, not die.

"On a regular basis I pray this: 'Lord, thank you so much for what you've done in this church in the past. Thank you for what you're doing now. And thank you for what you are going to continue to do in the future.'"

Exegete the Community: Wornall Road's Story

In October 2005 I was just starting to get a vision for how God could use my church planting experience to help the struggling churches around me in Kansas City. That's when I got a chance to put my newfound convictions concerning reclaiming the glory of God in our neighborhoods to the test. A group of older ladies from one of our city's once large and prominent churches, Wornall Road Baptist Church, visited my office. Like so many other churches in North America, the neighborhood surrounding it had changed vastly over the previous few decades, but the church hadn't changed with it. As a result, attendance had dwindled. The congregation had become virtually irrelevant to the community around it. Unless something changed quickly, the church would have to close its doors.

"Can you keep our church from closing?" they asked.

I knew the answer wasn't just to help them survive. As Erwin McManus so clearly described in his book *An Unstoppable Force,* "Once survival becomes our goal, we have lost our way." He goes on to explain: "The purpose of the church cannot be to survive, or even thrive, but to serve. And sometimes servants die in serving."[4]

I wanted this church to bring God glory through serving. Even if they were going to die, I wanted them to die in serving, not conserving—holding onto the last nickel to pay the last bill. During the next weeks and months I prepared the eighteen remaining members of the church for what would be coming next. We wouldn't close the church. We wouldn't change the name. But the church would need to make dramatic changes in order to reverse its course. We would need to suspend the church's constitution. (At this point, it made little sense anyway with fewer than twenty people in the church.) For the next six months, a team of three—myself and two other church members—would make all the decisions in the church short of closing the church or selling the property. We would treat the church as a new church start.

What did I do? First, I loved the older people who were in the church. I didn't make them the scapegoat for all the problems of the church. I didn't try to push them out of the church. I didn't ask them to be the change agents. I just loved them as the bride of Christ and tried to warm their hearts toward the gospel. Instead of telling them about all the changes we needed to make, I lifted up Jesus and what he did for us on the cross. I had them recount their conversion experiences. I did whatever I could to make much of

Jesus. I began immediately to preach gospel-saturated messages by taking them verse-by-verse through the text. If they were in fact converted, the preaching of the gospel would have an impact upon them.

At the same time, I did the work of the church planter, just as if I were starting a brand new church in the neighborhood. I invested in people's lives. I met people for coffee. I shared Christ with people and discipled them in the truths of the gospel.

In my process of sharing Christ with and discipling new people, I focused on young men between the ages of eighteen and thirty-five. I made the process of finding, evangelizing, discipling, and training the next generation of Wornall leaders one of the highest priorities of each day.

I then began to serve the community with abandon. When our neighborhood had looked at Wornall in recent years, they had seen a big building that didn't connect much with the surrounding neighborhood.

I did these two separate jobs—pastor of Wornall and initiator of what would become a brand-new church—simultaneously. This wasn't by any means a quick fix. It took time. It took work. It took a lot of prayer. But over time God began to bring new life to that old church.

We saw God redeem the building that had housed Wornall, and it became an active demonstration of the gospel to the community. What the neighboring community had once seen as a dead church that was not connected to the neighborhood, they began to see as a thriving hub for ministry. In the next few years following Wornall's relaunch, nine church plants used our building. At times we had up to four church plants in the building at one time. We did everything in our power to make Wornall an incubator for new churches.

The Wornall building became a happening place. With multiple churches meeting in the location at a time, something was always going on. Several nonprofit organizations used the building. In time, we rarely had vacancies. We used every room. On weekends the parking lot was full. It was a good problem to have because it showed our community that God was up to something in a building they for years had passed over for dead.

Not only did the building come alive, but the congregation did, too. Wornall became a visual illustration of the gospel message I preached from the pulpit every week. Neighborhoods like ours see businesses and organizations close their doors and move out of the area all the time. The stories of cities in North

America over the past sixty to seventy years have been fairly uniform. Though many have begun to rebound in recent years, they endured a massive transition in their sociological and economic makeup after World War II. Small businesses and nonprofit organizations (most notably churches) that could no longer connect with the changing demographics around them simply died or moved away.

Wornall showed something else to the community. The centerpiece of the gospel is that through the death of Jesus, God brought the opportunity for new life to the whole world (see Rom. 5:17). From the first pages of the Bible through the last, God consistently brings life to what is dead. Our neighborhood saw that at Wornall. It saw the gospel at work.

If Wornall had closed its doors in 2005, our neighborhood wouldn't have missed it. It would have been just another disconnected, dying institution in a neighborhood that had seen its share of losses over the past five decades. Today, that couldn't be further from the truth. If Wornall died or moved to the suburbs, I know our community would miss us.

Hundreds of students at both the high school and grade school would not receive meals each week. A maternity home and a family counseling center that serves our city would no longer be there. A local high school football team would have no one to provide cleats, first-aid kits, and sports banquets. That's just a partial list. Wornall impacts far more people every week than the number who gather for worship each week. To God's glory the community has become dependent on the ministry of Wornall.

In fall 2014, I turned over the pulpit of Wornall to a younger pastor who would lead the church into its next exciting stage of ministry. In the previous decade under my leadership, the church had grown from eighteen people to around one hundred fifty. Most important, our church had influenced the community in profound ways. Our neighborhood was noticeably better because God had resurrected a declining Wornall Road Baptist Church.

Simplify Your Strategy: First Baptist Church of Sachse's Story

When God called Josh King to First Baptist Church of Sachse, Texas, the church's best days had long since passed. Just looking at the church's facilities clearly illustrated this point. Though a large and once-thriving campus, the buildings needed numerous repairs. For example, the air conditioners and heaters needed to be replaced. Every roof was covered by a tarp. Those tarps had been up so long they were frayed.

But the dilapidated buildings masked bigger problems. Every week the church needed $11,000 to make budget, yet only $7,000 in tithes and offerings usually came in. Overworked and frustrated, the staff struggled to keep up with the overwhelming demands and limited resources inherent in how the church had been doing ministry for years.

The church of one hundred to one hundred twenty-five mostly senior adults had few visitors either. Maybe the most telling illustration of the church's decline came early in King's pastorate at the church. During a staff meeting one day, King asked the rest of the team what they did when visitors filled out a welcome card. The response from one staff member was candid: "Pastor, we haven't had a visitor in three years. You can do whatever you want with the cards."

Though obviously hyperbolic, it demonstrated a frustrating truth—visitors were the exception rather than the rule at this Texas church.

Like most other plateaued or dying churches, FBC Sachse's structure made growth and ministry effectiveness nearly impossible. Though having only a few more than one hundred attendees on most weekends, the church had programming like that of a church two

to three times its size. The church had three full services complete with preaching, music, children's ministry, and offerings every week. It had a full AWANA
program, children's choir, Vacation Bible School, and
Mother's Day Out, as well.

The overworked staff had begun to take the
church's failures personally. Frustrated and worn out
by the excessive programming, the staff had little hope
in the church's ability to move forward. To make matters worse, the staff felt the need to make the programs
look stronger than they were instead of letting struggling programs die a natural death.

One of the most striking examples of excessive programming came with the church's AWANA
program. When King became the church's pastor,
AWANA was bringing in large numbers of children
on Wednesday nights. But curiously, few of the parents were attending the church. When King asked
the staff person responsible for the program where
all the parents were, he was told they were attending a campus of a local megachurch. Evidently the
megachurch had Wednesday night community groups
but no children's programming on that night. So the
parents would drop their kids off at First Baptist and
attend their church's community groups. This meant
that staff and volunteers had to pour themselves into

STORIES OF TRANSFORMATION

a large program that ate resources—both time and money—but did little to help the church make disciples of families who attended the church on a regular basis.

The church's Vacation Bible School program had a similar problem. Large and time consuming, the ministry mostly drew children from other churches. When the church sent out a survey asking VBS attendees whether they attended another church and how many other VBS events they had participated in that summer, it became clear that they weren't reaching anyone new. For the most part, they were serving families who were already plugged into other local churches.

But those two ministries were just the tip of the iceberg. Most of the church's programming had very few attendees yet cost a great deal in time and money. Programs didn't die because the church wouldn't let them die. The death of a program typically brought with it the wrath of a longtime member, and everyone wanted to avoid that at all costs.

It didn't take King long to realize that streamlining the church's ministry offerings had to happen before meaningful change would be possible. King started by giving the staff permission to let the programs about which they weren't passionate die. The plan was simple. Instead of ending some of these ministries outright, he pulled the staff out of them and encouraged the congregation to run the ministries if they wanted them to continue. Most of the time, volunteers didn't step up, and the ministries died.

For King, explaining the logic of the necessary transition helped. Most established churches began by starting worship services, and as the church grew they added different small groups (or Sunday school classes) and ministries. When a church has shrunk in attendance, it has to start over in this process.

"When a church is only running one hundred, it doesn't make sense for them to do the programs they were doing when they were running eight hundred," King said. "You can't put in a quarter of what you were putting in and still expect to get the same amount."

Today, the church prides itself on being a "simple, relational church." They have small groups, a worship service, a simple women's ministry, a simple youth ministry, a simple children's ministry, and a simple benevolence ministry, and that's it. The bulky programs that wore out the staff and drained the church of resources for years are gone.

Now a church that had 100 to 125 most weeks before King's arrival just a few short years ago averages around 380 people each week. The church sent out more than 150 people to serve the community in

April 2015. All the needed repairs to the building have been made.

The church is in a much better place financially, too, thanks to the massive simplification process, than it was at the beginning of the transition. Besides being in the hole $4,000 every week, the church had no savings whatsoever when King became the church's pastor. Today the church has more than $160,000 on hand. Recently, it added three new staff members and raised the weekly budget by $2,000. The church also now pays all church staff at or above the national averages for their positions.

Despite the massive simplification that took place at FBC Sachse over the past few years, not every battle needed to be fought. In fact, King suggested, new leaders should pick well their battles.

"I'm very wary of revitalizers who make changes arbitrarily," King said. "There are so many guys who fight fights that shouldn't be fought and stress themselves out over changes that don't matter. Don't get all upset. Just lead. People will follow."

Focus on Reaching Young Men and Make Disciples Who Make Disciples: Calvary Church's Story

To illustrate where new churches are needed in Denver, and other cities throughout North America as well, you need to use a popular breakfast food—a doughnut. You have the hip, cool inner-city center where a number of new churches have rushed in during the last few years to start exciting new churches. Then you've got the mostly wealthy and white suburbs outside the doughnut where church planters have flocked in recent years looking for socioeconomic demographics that more match their backgrounds. But 70 percent of the city's population lives in the low-income, highly diverse doughnut that lies between.

As a Denver youth minister, God began to open Mark Hallock's eyes to the spiritual emptiness in Denver's doughnut. Not only were few church planters braving the doughnut to start new churches, but there was an abundance of church buildings that had once housed thriving churches now sitting mostly empty.

Hallock couldn't help but wonder, "Who is going to reach people in the doughnut?" He couldn't shake the answer. God was calling him to the work and to serve one of the struggling churches in the area.

That's when a friend introduced Hallock to Calvary Church in Englewood, Colorado. The church, nearly sixty years old at the time, was on life support and had only thirty people in attendance most weekends. The prognosis seemed clear to everyone: either God would step in and save the church, or it would surely die.

When Hallock became the church's pastor, he and the remaining members made a priority of three commitments. They would love their neighbors authentically. They would share the gospel each and every week. And they would preach through the Bible verse-by-verse.

From his days as a youth minister, Hallock had seen many boys—and later young men—who hadn't been mentored well. The same was true when he arrived at Calvary.

Realizing that behind every strong church you will always find strong male leaders, Hallock focused on mentoring young men. At the time, the church had a fairly traditional Southern Baptist structure with a senior pastor and several deacons. The new pastor began his mentoring effort with those few deacons, pouring his life into them and modeling what it means to lead.

"I'm not just talking about logistical leadership," Hallock said. "In many of our churches we're great at getting men involved when it comes to fixing a broken pipe or mowing the lawn. I'm talking about spiritual leadership, modeling a love for Jesus and our families."

Hallock continued to invest in the church's deacon body, which grew over time as the church grew. Eventually, the church transitioned to including both elders and deacons. Elders focused on using their pastoral gifts to attend to the church's spiritual needs. Deacons used their gifts of serving to help meet the growing congregation's physical needs. Today the church has eight elders, about twenty deacons, three deacons-in-training, and about eight elders-in-training.

Hallock noted that, "Everywhere you look now on Sunday morning you'll find men who are leading and serving the body."

Intentional one-on-one discipleship has become a way of life for Hallock and Calvary Church. Hallock realized that the church had one specific strength when he arrived and began connecting with the thirty who still called Calvary home. The remaining members didn't have the luxury of serving in ministry silos. There was no youth worship service or children's worship service or senior adult ministry. They were one church.

Hallock wanted to use the church's natural multi-generational character to its advantage. He looked for ways to better connect young and old so they could share their lives and hear one another's stories. That became the heartbeat of the church's DNA groups. These multigenerational groups of two to four men and two to four women meet weekly for encouragement, prayer, and Bible study. The church has community groups where families and such gather for fellowship and the DNA groups provide the significant discipleship.

By far the most significant chapter in Calvary's recent journey came during a 2010 retreat. It became evident early on to Hallock that two streams of the congregation were developing. The first stream, the thirty people who were already attending when Hallock first took the pulpit, was Calvary 1.0. The second stream, the thirty people who had joined the church since his arrival, was Calvary 2.0.

Although Hallock realized that those who made up Calvary 1.0 were excited about all God was doing in their midst, they still were facing many changes in the church they had grown to love throughout the years. Calvary 2.0 shared the excitement, but they knew little of the church's history that the other stream took for granted.

As the two streams gathered for the first evening of the retreat, Hallock gathered everyone into a circle and talked first to Calvary 1.0.

"I told that first group, look, you guys have been so faithful to this church for years, some of you have been here for fifty years," Hallock said. "Can you spend some time over the next few hours telling us the stories of Calvary?" So they did—story after story. Some made you cry. Others made you laugh. All were inspiring.

The next morning Hallock asked the Calvary 2.0 group, "Why do you want to be a part of this church? Why are you here?" Time after time, the longtime members of the church heard new attendees talk about how much they appreciated the work the church had done in the community. They now wanted to invest their lives in the neighborhood, and they couldn't wait to see what God would do through this church in the years to come. As the two groups shared, the Holy Spirit brought unity.

That Saturday afternoon the two groups came together as Calvary 3.0 to dream about what God would do in the future.

Six years into the replanting efforts at Calvary Church, the thirty regulars from Calvary 1.0 have turned into seven hundred regular attenders in Calvary 3.0. And it's clear that God is still on the move.

"We're still 92 percent lost in this city," Hallock said. "We want to penetrate neighborhoods with incarnational ministry and the love of Jesus, the power of the gospel, and a shepherding philosophy that really cares about people and families."

CHAPTER 6

DEFINING SUCCESS

How you define success in a replanting effort can determine how you go about the process. Early success may be as simple as stopping the bleeding and stabilizing the patient. It can also include the very beginning steps toward creating a hunger for biblical truth among the remaining members while warming their hearts toward the gospel.

If your congregation doesn't believe the replant is successful until you have a thousand people attending each weekend or until you are the biggest church in town, you will burn out long before you get there. The age of the megachurch has been tough on struggling churches. We tend to look at what large churches are doing and assume large numbers equal the blessing of

God. Most of us intuitively realize that's not true, but subconsciously we buy into the lie without even realizing it.

Numbers alone are an inadequate barometer of a replanted church's transformation. I never call a church small. A church of fewer than two hundred in gathered worship is not small. It's normative. It's only "small" when compared to the very small number of very large churches.

Below are statistics from the 2013 SBC Annual Church Profile regarding SBC churches:

- 1–99 attendees = 25,217 churches (62.7%)
- 100–199 attendees = 8,305 churches (20.7%)
- 200–299 attendees = 2,850 churches (7.1%)
- 300–499 attendees = 2,126 churches (5.3%)
- 500–749 attendees = 788 churches (2.0%)
- 750–999 attendees = 336 churches (0.8%)
- 1,000–1,999 attendees = 425 churches (1.1%)
- 2,000+ attendees = 139 churches (0.3%)

Churches having fewer than two hundred people in attendance are normative, not small. The vast, vast majority of churches throughout church history have been of fewer than two hundred people. It's time our expectations matched reality.

If my daughter-in-law takes my grandson to the doctor and is told he is in the 90th percentile for height and weight, she doesn't then assume he's too small simply because 10 percent of boys his age are bigger. The same is true for churches. We need to stop measuring the effectiveness of a congregation, particularly a replanted one, by the largest 10 percent of churches. Those expectations will doom the potential of the replanting process before it even begins. With the likelihood being very small that a church will ever grow beyond two hundred, the church that makes becoming a megachurch its goal will give up way too early.

I am most certainly not saying anything negative about megachurches. I praise God every day for their ministries and the impact they have had on North America and on my life. Without the growth of megachurches in the past few decades, the baptism rates and church-to-population rates that have distressed us all in the past few years would have fallen off a cliff. Megachurches are not the problem. Let me reiterate that. Megachurches are not the problem. Do you hear me, pastor of a normative-sized church? Do you think the reason you can't grow is because of the megachurches and their various ministry offerings? The problem occurs when you as a normative-sized church try to emulate the ministry of a megachurch.

You need to discover the community to which God has called you and design a ministry to reach and minister to that community. Think of a megachurch as an aircraft carrier and your normative-sized church as a PT boat in World War II. Both were important, and both had very different roles to play in the battle. We need all sizes of churches for the battle in which we are engaged.

Dr. John Marshall, lead pastor at Second Baptist Church in Springfield, Missouri (one of the largest churches in the state of Missouri), once shared with me that he and his pastoral peers as young men looked up to Dr. Jerry Falwell as a role model in many aspects of his ministry, including his commitment to biblical preaching and evangelism. But they also looked to him as a role model in planting what we now call the megachurch. Marshall said that he and his peers believed that if they could plant large, Bible-believing churches in every city in North America, they would make a profound difference in our nation. While deeply grateful for the incredible ministry of many megachurches, Marshall noted that we have obviously failed to reach the nation despite their incredible proliferation in the past few decades.

We have more megachurches in the city of Nashville, Tennessee, alone today than we had in all of North America during the 1970s, yet we are further behind in baptisms and nearly every other evangelistic metric available to us than we were at that time. And as the number of megachurches has grown in recent decades, we have lost a tremendous number of vibrant, healthy neighborhood churches that were invested in their community. Many churches that averaged two hundred only a few decades ago now regularly have thirty or fewer.

My own Southern Baptist Convention remains a denomination of mostly churches of fewer than two hundred in attendance. If all the pastors who preached to two hundred or less each Sunday packed into Royals Stadium in Kansas City, it would nearly fill the stadium. More than thirty-three thousand pastors stand before congregations of less than two hundred each week. You could put all the SBC pastors who preach to more than one thousand people each week in one jumbo jet. There aren't enough "big" churches to reach North America. But imagine what might happen if the forty-thousand-plus normative-sized churches became culturally relevant, gospel-saturated, disciple-making centers throughout North America. Now we are talking about a game changer.

The Only Metric That Matters

That takes us to the only metric that really matters as a replanted church. If numbers can't tell the appropriate story, what can? Here's a secret. The only metric that matters can't be measured entirely from within your church walls. Jesus gives us this metric in the Great Commission. Our job is to make disciples who make disciples. You may be asking, "Isn't that measured within the church building? Can't I measure our replanted church's disciple-making prowess by how many people attend gathered worship or even the numbers involved in small groups?"

Not a chance. Remember what Paul told Timothy in his second letter to the young pastor? "All Scripture is inspired by God and is profitable for teaching, for rebuking, for correcting, for training in righteousness, so that the man of God may be complete, equipped for every good work" (2 Tim. 3:16–17). As critical as reading, learning, and memorizing biblical truth is to our disciple-making as churches, it can't measure our success. Paul tells us that the point of Scripture is to equip God's people for good work.

Making disciples who make disciples must lead to a transformed neighborhood around the church. While this kind of metric frees us from an over reliance on numbers, it also raises the bar significantly as

112

far as discipleship. Instead of attendance, let's think of decreased crime in the neighborhood, improved schools, and an increase in intact families. No, the neighborhood surrounding your church will never reach perfection this side of eternity, but I have seen firsthand that normative-sized, replanted neighborhood churches can impact communities in amazing ways. Progress will be slow, but it will come.

Replanting leaders must continually remind their congregations of what truly matters as they go through this process. You have to preach it. You have to share it over coffee. You have to make it clear in every venue possible. Doing this pushes the focus of the congregation outward, reminding members why they are enduring the pain necessary at various points in the replanting process. It will also give the congregation the courage to keep moving forward in times when attendance and other typical metrics aren't rebounding as quickly as some would like.

CHAPTER 7

AM I A REPLANTER?

In 1987 my first assignment as a new (and very young) national denominational leader for church planting was to set up a booth at a missions conference for students in Atlanta, Georgia. At the conference, students from all over North America were supposed to sign up for how they wanted to serve in their stints as two-year missionaries right out of college. I sat in that church-planting booth for an entire day without anyone coming to my booth. All the students were flooding the community ministry, student ministry, and resort ministry booths instead. No one knew what church planting was. I had to personally recruit students to draw any interest in church planting. Today, that dynamic has totally shifted. Show up on any seminary campus and the largest crowds will likely be drawn to hear from church planters and to learn how to become a planter.

A couple of years after my initial (failed) experience in Atlanta trying to recruit students to plant churches, a national missions magazine featured a young Southern California church planter who was seeing amazing results outside the Bible Belt by speaking directly to spiritual seekers. That article on Saddleback Church founding pastor, Rick Warren, represented the early embers in a new movement of young leaders moving toward church planting in SBC circles and beyond. In recent years the popularity has reached a crescendo. Go into a Southern Baptist seminary today and many young leaders would prefer to start a new church rather than deal with problems in an established church. Many have been convinced that to be truly an up-and-coming young leader in the broader SBC world, they need to go plant a church first. Even leaders who clearly aren't called to start churches have been caught up in the wave, often having disappointing results when they reach the mission field.

I pray for a day when we also see thousands of young men around our convention answering God's call to replant churches. I pray for that day because the need is so clear right now. We have declining and dying churches in every corner of our continent. We have resources not being tapped and people not being mobilized because these churches lie dormant. Though we need many more church planters to push back lostness throughout North America, we can't miss the opportunity to replant dying churches either.

Over the past two decades, many of our high-capacity Christian leaders have become church planters. Again, as a former church planter myself, I find this incredibly encouraging. I applaud wholeheartedly the trend. But as encouraging as that has been, I am now seeing great high-capacity leaders expressing a desire to replant dying churches. This is something I have never seen before in these kinds of numbers. It is an answer to prayer before our very eyes.

This is a time to move forward. Dying churches need high-capacity leaders. We need to proclaim this from our pulpits and teach this in our seminaries. We need to lift up and honor the talented crop of church leaders who are now tackling and thriving in these tough ministry situations.

Clearly, not everyone is called to replant dying churches. In fact, some who are called into church planting aren't called into replanting. Some who are called into pastoring local churches aren't called to be replanters either. Replanting requires gifts and skills that are both a mixture of church planting and pastoring and, at times, completely unique as well.

What are some of the characteristics I look for when assessing prospective replanting pastors? Of course, I look for young men who meet the biblical qualifications outlined in the New Testament. They are able to teach, lead their families, remain faithful to their wives, manage their money, be in high repute throughout the neighborhood, and all the other characteristics outlined in Scripture.

A replanter must have a passion for biblical preaching. He doesn't need to be the next Martin Lloyd Jones, but he must have a love for doctrinally rich, Christ-centered preaching. Through consistent preaching of the gospel, cold hearts will be warmed. Most Southern Baptists, even those in dying churches, will tell you that they believe the Bible to be true. The replanter must start with the Bible and stay with the Bible.

It is also imperative that the replanter be a man of prayer. Many times he will be driven to his knees crying out to God for his intervention in what seems to be a hopeless situation. Prayer is our primary weapon in defeating the enemy and breaking his stronghold. At Wornall, our replant really began to emerge when two young men, Kumar and Brian, asked to meet me late on Thursday evenings to pray. Soon the three of us became four and then five. A consistent prayer life is without a doubt the single most important aspect in the life of a replanter.

It is also critical that replanting pastors demonstrate other specific characteristics. I work with some great replanting coaches, and we have developed the following list of eight characteristics that we believe are necessary in the making or breaking of a potential replanting candidate.

He must be a visionary shepherd. Any successful replanter must demonstrate the ability to walk a fine line between being a man of mission and a loving shepherd to those whom God has entrusted to him. Like other leaders, replanters can't wait around for someone to tell them what to do next. And there isn't a turnkey program you can work to replant. Instead, you will need to understand how God can give you a vision for your life, your church, and your community and be able to communicate that vision to others so they can take hold of it and own it, too.

But here is where the roles of a church planter and a church replanter diverge. As a church planter, your initial members will obviously embrace your vision; otherwise, they wouldn't be part of your new plant. However, in the case of replanting, that is not necessarily true. Many remaining members will be there just because they have always been there. You will have to shepherd their hearts toward your vision if you expect them to get on board.

Sheep won't move in a certain direction just because you tell them that is where they should go. They follow you because of the trust you have built with them. That only happens after you have spent time with them as their pastor, loving them, discipling them, and caring about what matters to them.

Biblical preaching is foundational to visionary shepherding. As you shepherd the church's remaining members, you will need to deliver doctrinally sound, gospel-saturated sermons. Visionary leadership for the church's future will require prophetic preaching as well. As the visionary shepherd, you are the primary change agent for the congregation. You will have to learn to manage change in a way that continues to lead your people toward our Lord's vision for his church while not moving so far and fast ahead of them that they lose sight of you and the vision. Neither do you want to move so slowly that you miss the windows of opportunity for change. You will need to become adept at learning how your particular flock responds to change. You will have to become an expert at how members process information and how they arrive at decisions. As you shepherd them you are moving them toward the vision of glorifying God in their context as they make disciples who make disciples that result in the community being noticeably better.

Your success as a visionary shepherd will be directly in proportion to your personal and intimate love relationship with Jesus. Without spending considerable time in prayer and fellowship with your Savior, you cannot be a visionary shepherd. You become a visionary shepherd as you spend time with the Good Shepherd and begin to acquire his heart for the flock he has entrusted to you. If you struggle to love your people, it is because you are struggling in your love for Jesus. The more you love Jesus, the more you will love your people.

He must have a high tolerance for pain. Replanting a dying church isn't easy—far from it, in fact. Pain is a certainty for any replanting pastor. The adversary has staked a claim on every dying church across North America. He won't give up the church without a fight. A new replanter once asked me what to expect in the early days of the replant. I responded from my heart and my own experience, "You can expect periods of deep discouragement and depression followed by every personal, financial, and family struggle you can imagine, and then it gets hard." Replanting a church is not an adventure or a journey. It is a battle, straight up.

As I watch National Hockey League players, I am amazed at their tolerance for pain. I admire their ability to play through the pain. I watched one example of this ability to play through pain on live television during the Stanley Cup play-offs in 2013. Gregory Campbell played for more than a minute with a broken leg to help his team, the Boston Bruins, kill a penalty. That is "taking one" for the team. Replanting a church will require you to play through the pain. A replanting pastor who does not have a high tolerance for pain and discomfort won't push through the tough times. Playing through the pain does not depend upon your own mental or emotional toughness, but rather on your ability to embrace the cross and the gospel in such a way that they sustain and strengthen you.

The cross itself must be what propels us forward through this pain. As replanters we must share Paul's assertion in Philippians 3:10: "My goal is to know Him and the power of His resurrection and the fellowship of His sufferings, being conformed to His death." That is what gets us through the inevitable pain that comes with replanting. When you understand that the suffering you are enduring in replanting a dying church is ultimately for the glory of God, then the suffering has a purpose and can become an act of worship. The pain can then become meaningful and, in a sense, a joy in your life.

He must have a love for the local church and an affinity for its history. Replanting pastors must demonstrate a commitment to and a love for the local church, with all its scars, wounds, and dysfunction. A decade ago this was tough to find. Many young Christian leaders were done with the local church. Not only were they ready to give up on the dying church, but they thought the old building would be a deterrent to the unchurched. Church planters in the mainstream were looking to plant churches in "non-church" settings. This, too, has changed. Today many young church planters understand the beauty of a "sacred" structure within a neighborhood. They also value the repurposing of the building as a responsible use of resources.

I am excited that in very recent years I am seeing an ever-increasing number of young leaders who don't just love the *idea* of church, they love the local, dying church itself. They see her potential and her biblical role in God's mission, and they run to it, not away from it. They understand the importance of raising again the banner of God's glory over the dying church. The narrative about dying churches is changing. Many young men now see reclaiming a dying church as an opportunity to be embraced rather than a danger to be avoided.

This kind of love for the irreplaceable individuals who make up that church requires that a replanting pastor have an appreciation of the church's history and the history of the community in which it is planted. When you appreciate a church's history, you will try to discover more about how it got started, why it got started, and who started it. You will also want to learn when the church was most effective in reaching its neighborhood and making much of God. Celebrate the stories of God at work in the church's past with the remaining members so they can understand that you are building on a legacy of missions and ministry in the neighborhood that has long been part of the congregation.

He must be a resourceful generalist. As you begin to replant, be ready to tackle any and every aspect of church life. When I arrived at Wornall, I not only planned the worship service, I wrote, printed, and folded the worship bulletin. I led worship with an MP3 player. I came early to be sure the restrooms had supplies. I filled the first-time guest bags. I checked the pressure in the boiler. I learned how to restart the air conditioner. I located a sound system to borrow and found a friend from another church to come and run sound for a while. My wife and I cleaned out the preschool area and set up a new nursery as best we could. If you don't know how to do something that needs to be done, it is your job in the early stages of the replant to learn how to do it or to find a ministry partner to help you do it.

Become aware of the myriad resources and information that are available to you through your denomination, networks, and partnerships. Ask lots of questions and become a focused learner.

Not accomplishing things that need to be done is not an option. You cannot have the attitude of "that's not my job." If there is no one else to do it (or no one you would want to do it) then *you* have to do it. In fact, as you tackle many different tasks, you develop an appreciation for those in your flock who eventually will take on these responsibilities. Serving in a variety of capacities creates in us humility. It reveals to your people that you have a servant's heart. Never, never let them hear you complain about serving. Trust me, they will model that behavior in a heartbeat. Let them see that you find joy in serving.

However, let me be very quick to say that from the outset you are seeking other people to pick up these tasks. You cannot create an environment where you do all the work and the people let you do it. That serves no purpose. Rather, you need to be ready, willing, and eager to do what needs to be done without complaining, all the while shepherding them and then trusting them as they make the ministry their own. In this way you model not only a joyful servant's heart, but also you model how to reproduce yourself in others.

As your church grows, your measure of success is making disciples who make disciples who make the community noticeably better. As you teach others how to perform tasks and then pass those tasks off to them, you are modeling for them how they, too, can create leaders. Embrace the season of being a resourceful generalist as an opportunity to model a servant's heart and a formula for reproducing leadership.

He must have an aptitude for serving in multigenerational contexts. Effective replanting pastors can minister to and minister with people from a variety of generations. A Christian leader who can work only with middle-aged and elderly church members will never be able to infuse the church with the young leaders needed to turn around a declining church. Conversely, a leader who can only work with young people will never be able to gain the leadership capital needed to make transformative change in the church and community. Replanting leaders who effectively mobilize multiple generations in a church will model to their neighborhoods a church family who leaves no one out and seeks to involve everyone in the mission of God.

Chief among the many things we can identify about the first-century church recorded in the New Testament is the fact that they were a multigenerational church. Paul instructs Timothy concerning his youth and his leadership skills. He guides young Timothy through the process of respectfully correcting the older men. Instructions are given to young women and older women and to young men and older men. In most churches today, however, especially in most church plants, very few older people are present. In most dying churches very few younger people are present. The church is a family, and it should be comprised of all generations.

A church consisting of many generations is uncommon and can be difficult to manage because of the effort required. Satan fully knows the powerful testimony a multigenerational church will have upon a self-centered world, and he uses all the weaknesses of our flesh to work against us as we seek to embrace generations unlike ours. In our sinful human nature, we grow weary with trying to relate to people who see the world, make decisions, and process information differently than we do. Furthermore, technology has in some ways exacerbated the problem by changing the way we socialize, replacing face-to-face interactions with cold, impersonal digital experiences. Older saints who don't embrace or understand technology can be left behind completely in this new way of communicating.

It takes work to love and understand each other. People of all generations must subordinate their desires and preferences for the glory of God and the advancement of his kingdom. We have to think less of ourselves and much more of God and the gospel. We have to *live* the gospel, not just sing about, talk about, and read about it. When we battle our flesh and embrace self-sacrifice for the sake of the kingdom, we discover joy that is far deeper than the joy of having things our own way.

Even in a church having a variety of generations, a pull exists toward separating the generations within the gathered church. Various generations need to worship and serve together. I grew up in a very program-based church, and the only time my family spent together on Sunday mornings was our time in the car. As soon as we hit the door of the church, we were all funneled into our own environments of age-graded Bible study and worship. Often churches that have multiple worship services will design one for the older members and another for the younger ones. All of this generational segregation tends to reinforce our desire to consider our particular age group as the one that matters most.

While a place exists for age-appropriate learning within the church, much also is to be learned by young children as they observe older children and adults worshiping and serving. It is good for adults to rejoice when small children and infants are with their parents in worship and during activities of the church. The noise of children in worship is cause for rejoicing. Accommodating the needs of generations other than our own serves to remind us that "it is not about us." God alone should be the desire of our hearts, and we can more fully embrace and enjoy him when we think less of ourselves. The disciples tried generational segregation, and Jesus would have none of it. "Leave the children alone, and don't try to keep them from coming to Me" (Matt. 19:14).

The struggle to embrace a different generation goes both ways. Older people must find joy in passing leadership to the next generation. They must learn to find joy in witnessing the next generation infusing the gospel into their context. They must let go of the idol of the past, their need to control and, most important, their need to be made much of for all the work they have put in through the years. They need to rejoice in all the work Jesus has done for them through the years. The younger people likewise need to identify the real and meaningful struggles older people endure. As we age, we all will endure a constant sense of loss as we lose careers, loved ones, mobility, and even control of our lives. Older people are fully aware that they face one day losing their independence, becoming more and more dependent on others. Young people need to show an overwhelming amount of compassion to older people and walk with them through this difficult stage in life. As we focus more and more on the beauty, perfection, and complete satisfaction that is our Bridegroom, we will embrace the reality that all of us who are in this church are his bride—from the very young to the very old, all are his bride.

Potential replanters should examine their past history of working with older people. It would be helpful to take any course available at your local community college on understanding the geriatric population. Learn how they process information and how they come to decisions. Spend time with older people by volunteering in various organizations or clubs that are populated with lots of older folks. Recently my wife volunteered with our local genealogical society and discovered that nearly all the members were twice her age. They were thrilled to have a young person among them. Find ways to engage the older generation and discover how adept you are at communicating and connecting. If you can't work with older people, or if young people do not respond to your leadership, and if you are not passionate about seeing all generations represented in your church, then replanting is not for you.

He must have tactical patience. When you start your journey as a replanting pastor, you will likely come into a situation that requires quite a bit of change in order to move the church forward. The church may (and likely will) need updates to the facility, new governing documents, a refreshed worship experience, a new website, and a variety of other changes regarding how church is done. A replanting pastor must know what needs to be changed and when. You cannot and should not change everything at once.

You will have to exhibit great patience in not rushing through just to check changes off your list. Instead, you will need to make changes at the right time, in the right place, and for the right reasons. In a replanting situation, you will want to make changes when the church as a whole has bought into the decision, and it has become "their" decision.

A replanter must realize that this is not a short-term mission trip; this is his life. As you have likely heard before, we tend to underestimate what we can do in a lifetime and overestimate what we can do in a year. You must be patient and not give in to the pressure of changing the vision before you are finished. But neither can you rush through the necessary changes. A replanting pastor knows what needs to be changed first, what can wait, and what likely doesn't need to be changed, though he may prefer some things be done differently.

Having spent most of my ministry as a church planter, I was accustomed to a fast-paced style of leadership and ministry. When I wasn't planting churches, I was in denominational leadership roles coaching planters. I knew that the first three years of a church plant were by far the most critical. If you didn't gain some serious traction and momentum in the first three years, your chance of doing so in the subsequent years was greatly diminished.

In church planting you move ahead with extreme focus and accelerate as you go. You set the vision and keep it clear. You place people in leadership who are in agreement with that vision and the pace of the strategy. In replanting as well, you must set the vision and keep it clear. You must also move ahead, but the pace is likely going to be entirely different.

At Wornall Road I don't think we broke fifty in attendance for two or three years. Remember we were in a metropolitan setting. For a church plant in a metropolitan setting to have fewer than fifty in gathered worship after three years, experience tells me the future for that church plant is pretty bleak. In replanting, so much more had to be done before we realized any traction in numerical growth.

Among the matters to be attended are pastoral care and guidance of the remaining members who may be suffering some form of post-traumatic church stress disorder from previous bad experiences. One replanter compared his efforts to rescue a church from death to a lifeguard saving a panic-stricken swimmer. You may be saving him from drowning, but he will fight you all the way to the shore.

In-depth community exegesis and relationship building must also happen. Modeling discipleship to a few individuals over an extended period of time and leading them to make disciples must go forward as well. There may be issues with the building that need to be addressed and perhaps church governance and leadership structures that need to change.

During this time it is imperative that the replanter have a stubborn, yet loving ability to stay on message. He cannot become discouraged by taking a long (sometimes really long) on-ramp to get the church where it needs to be. Planters are often wired to effect change and see results quickly. Replanters need the same tenacity as planters in regard to focused leadership and clear vision, but they will need to be much more at ease with the slower pace needed to get there. There may be ministerial peer pressure to move things along faster. "You have been there two years, and you haven't increased attendance?" Questions such as that could discourage a replanter if he doesn't have a realistic view of the length of the on-ramp.

It is easy for the strategy and vision to move off target over time. The replanter has to be stubborn (Have I mentioned that before?) about the strategy and vision. When things are moving at a slow pace, there will always be those who want to jumpstart it with an "instant" program or emphasis. The replanter will need to be diligent and guard against such intrusions into the overarching strategy.

He must have a high emotional awareness. In order to replant a dying church, you must be aware of your own emotions and feelings. You must have a strong and solid sense of who you are in Christ. Because you are working in constantly changing situations and with diverse populations of people, you will need to be self-aware and get your identity through the gospel and not through your performance or the "positive" feedback you receive from those you lead.

Unfortunately, some people are drawn toward pastoral ministry because they feed off others. They seek their validation and worth in how their congregation reacts to them and responds to their ministry. A pastor of any kind—but particularly a replanting pastor—must feed his congregation, not *be fed by* his congregation. You will also need the ability to read people and to sum up quickly their strengths and weaknesses. You will need to know how to motivate and influence people without manipulating them. You have to be a great listener and observer of people. You will need the ability to defuse situations that need defusing. I have often seen leaders spend $10 on a 10¢ problem. At the same time, you need to know when a seemingly insignificant issue cannot be ignored because it will only grow worse. There will be times when you will need to be the glue that holds relationships together, and at other times you will need to be the oil that lubricates rough relationships. You cannot accomplish this if you are not secure in yourself through the gospel.

You will need to find your worth not in what your congregation gives you, but in what Jesus has already done for you. As a replanting pastor, you must be able to serve from the overflow of what God is doing in you through the gospel. When you have this strong sense of identity, you will be able to listen and interact with people free from a need to make them like you. That is critical for a replanting pastor. You may look at your peers and discover they are leading larger and seemingly more impactful churches. You may struggle for months or even years and have little to show for it if you are only counting the number in gathered worship. During such times it is critical that your sense of call, fulfillment, and purpose comes from Christ alone and his work for you and through you. I cannot say it often enough: if you need lots of positive feedback and constant affirmation from those you lead or from your peers, replanting may not be your calling.

He must have spousal support and clarity of call. Just as in any other ministry situation—whether you are a pastor, church planter, or a replanting pastor— your wife has to cooperate with both your call and sense her own call to your place of service. I believe this is even more critical for a replanting pastor. In a replanting situation, your wife will deal with the ghosts of all the previous pastors' wives. People will often project upon your wife some of the expectations and even the hurt they have experienced from previous pastors' wives. A church planter's wife often gets to define the role of pastor's wife for the church. The wife of a replanting pastor doesn't have that same luxury.

Your wife will need to realize that, as you seek to change the congregation's mind about its mission and role in the community, perceptions of the role of pastor's wife will likely change in the process. Unfortunately, that change won't happen overnight, and it won't happen without some level of difficulty and stress upon her. She needs to understand and sense her calling too in the endeavor, but you will need to provide support and help her find other support as you move through this process.

Replanters must have a strong understanding that God has called them to this task. It cannot be an experiment or a rung on the ladder to a bigger church. It must be a call to that church and to that community. You need to understand that your call is to both. There will be days, plenty of them in fact, when you will become so frustrated with the church that you will be tempted to walk away. Precisely during those moments will God's call on your life and your love of the community compel you to stay. If you have a tendency to find your worth in results, such as growth in numbers, then replanting is not for you. (I would suggest ministry in general is not for you.)

There were many Sundays in the early days at Wornall when I could have shot off a cannon in the sanctuary and not hit anyone. When you have thirty people in an auditorium that seats six hundred—I don't care who you are—that is a tough room. Replanters have to be so secure in who they are in Christ that their worth and value as a leader comes not from the results they see week-to-week but from what Christ *has* accomplished for them and *is* accomplishing for them every day.

Unfortunately, some insecure pastors exist who look to numbers to validate their worth. A replanter cannot be among them.

CHAPTER 8

YOU CAN'T REPLANT

You can't replant a church. For that matter, you can't plant a church either. Don't get me wrong. In order for a church to be replanted, you must do a tremendous amount of work. But *you* can't replant a church.

Do you recall Jesus' first miracle recorded in the Gospel of John? It was the wedding in Cana of Galilee. John records it in the second chapter of his Gospel.

There was a problem. They had run out of wine. Jesus told the servants to fill six large jars with water. Scripture says the servants filled the water jars to the brim. The problem at the wedding feast wasn't that they didn't have any water. The problem was that they didn't have any wine. But the servants did what servants do. They obeyed. These servants didn't just throw a little water into the jars. They put as much water in the jars as a jar could possibly hold. They filled them to the brim.

You and I know that Jesus didn't need the servants to put the water in the jars in order to create wine. He certainly could have created wine out of nothing. Jesus chose to use the servants' work as part of the plan to meet the need at the wedding feast. And that's the way it is with replanting the church. For God's glory and our joy, the Lord places us in a dying church and gives us lots of work to do. Like the servants who filled the jars to the brim, we also need to be diligent, strategic, and thorough in our work. God has decided that just as the servants' work in bringing the water to the jars was necessary, so our work in replanting is necessary. But just like the servants bringing water to the jars, our work alone is not effectual. All the obedient work the servants did strategically to fill those jars with water didn't solve the problem at the wedding. It was still just water in a jar.

For all the work we may do—community exegesis, learning how to work with older people, developing and mentoring young men, serving our community, repairing the building—none of that will replant a dying church. It was the effectual work of Jesus that turned ordinary water into the best wine. Likewise, it is the effectual work of the Holy Spirit in response to the repentance and prayers of the redeemed church of God that will defeat the enemy and replant a dying church.

Only the divine power of God, the glorious message of the gospel, and the effectual calling of the Holy Spirit in the lives of men and women will replant a dying church.

It is a privilege and an honor to be asked by our Lord to participate in the task of replanting his church. The fact that only his work is effectual in replanting should motivate us to fill the jars to the brim. In other words, we should do everything he tells us to do and be obedient in every aspect of our lives, and then we trust him to do that which only he can do. When we do that, we are just like the servants in the story. We get to witness firsthand the glory of our Lord.

What was the ultimate result when the servants did only what Jesus asked them to do, and then Jesus did what only he could do? Was it just great wine for a feast? No it was far more than that. John makes clear in the eleventh verse, "Jesus performed this first sign in Cana of Galilee. He displayed His glory, and His disciples believed in Him."

God received all the glory. I can think of no better activity in which to be involved than the work of replanting a dying church so that God can miraculously bring it back to life. When he does, he receives all the glory, and we have a front-row seat to see it all.

COUNTING THE COST TO REPLANT

As I was about to embark on my own replanting journey in 2012, I thought it wise to speak with men who had gone before me, men who were still standing, loving Jesus and their families, and were fully engaged in ministry.

After some twitter stalking, I was able to sit down with Mark Clifton over breakfast. He kindly grilled me about my plans, my vision for the church, and my philosophy of replanting. I survived the gauntlet and then had the privilege of asking him a few questions. Fortunately, I'd done my homework and had a few ready, so I asked first: "What can I expect during my first year of replanting?"

He paused, sat back, and then leaned toward me, responding with the seriousness one has when sharing deep and significant truths: "You can expect significant spiritual attack and deep, dark depression."

Mark provided a few accounts of his own experience, including this one I will never forget:

> One Sunday, after a particularly discouraging month and after battling for a few years with all my might to replant this church, the crowd was exceptionally small. Just moments before preaching, I had dealt with major conflict between older members and newer ones. That morning the sound system kept alternately cutting out and blaring feedback, and our music that day was about the worse I had ever remembered. I was struggling with my preaching so badly that morning, and I could see by the look in the eyes of my wife, my most ardent supporter, that even she was having a hard time listening. I was desperately trying to find a way to salvage this service and my sermon. I did my best to gather my thoughts, and just as I was about to bring the sermon in for a landing our steeple clarion unexpectedly

began to blare "A Mighty Fortress is our God"; so, I stopped the sermon mid-sentence, closed in prayer, walked out the back door during the last song, and kept on walking two blocks down the street and sat on the steps of a nearby high school.

In that moment of frustration, with tears and prayer, I confessed that I was ready to give up and move on; it didn't appear that God was going to change this church and I was beyond exhausted. At that point I looked down and noticed that I was still wearing the wireless microphone. It was at that moment that I sensed the voice of God saying to me, "You're not done here yet. And before I replant this church, I am reshaping you to depend on me and not your ability."

As Mark shared that story, my thoughts raced; the voice inside my head was saying, *Not me, this won't happen to me.* I tried to look interested but was ready to move on to the next question as quickly as possible—something to do with strategy, transitioning governance or some such topic. I thanked Mark for the advice and left that breakfast meeting without thinking much about his story.

The first three months of my replant weren't bad. There were a few bumps when I changed the bulletin, wore jeans on Sunday mornings, and when we began changing the worship style—but all in all, things were progressing; that is, *until* late January of 2013.

After sharing key observations from home visits and initial thoughts on strategy and future direction with my leadership team, things began to get difficult.

To name a few things:

- Secret meetings were held to discuss my leadership and our new direction.
- False reports and lies began circulating about our plans and actions.
- The first ever church discipline case resulted in a long time family leaving the church, followed by several of their close friends.
- Our youngest daughter began having nightmares regularly.
- I experienced frequent spiritual and demonic attacks at night.
- Mechanical breakdowns of all sorts (automobiles, appliances, computers) occurred in clusters.
- Financial challenges and setbacks—both personal and for the congregation—happened frequently.

- My older daughter wrecked her car (which had just been replaced).
- The core group who came with us to help replant the church experienced conflict and division, and some of them left.
- I sank into a deep, dark, and sustained depression.

The warnings I had received from Mark were prophetic. It had happened to me. If you're embarking on a replanting journey they'll likely happen to *you*.

Why?

A replanting pastor is seeking to reclaim ground for God's glory, ground that has been under enemy control for years, if not decades. Simply changing the music style, adding coffee, and putting a new sign out front won't win this ground. This ground is only won back through prayer, the power of the Holy Spirit, and the real hand-to-hand spiritual combat of pastoring people well.

Challenging the status quo isn't simply a ministry strategy issue; it's a heart issue. Comfort and preference are often loved more than Jesus. Dislodging this idolatry unleashes the wrath and fury of the one who desires to keep it there. To stop it, he will go after you, your family, your finances, and your health. He will attack the unity in the church; he will raise up adversaries.

You, like the apostle Paul, will be able to say, for *"we were completely overwhelmed—beyond our strength—so that we even despaired of life. Indeed, we personally had a death sentence within ourselves"* (2 Cor. 1:8–9, italics added).

In the mud and muck of replanting, you'll be pushed beyond your strength, you will despair, and you'll likely think you are going to die—if nothing changes.

Replanter, here is a purpose in our suffering: But, that was to make us rely not on ourselves but on God who raises the dead (see 2 Cor. 1:9).

As a replanter, it is easy to trust in your ability to persuade, your visioning skills or your finely tuned strategy. Here's the thing: God will let you do that, *until he doesn't.*

Suffering and hardship are designed to make us relinquish our propensity to rely on ourselves. The church you are seeking to replant has likely been relying on itself for years—this is why it needs to be replanted.

God does a work in the heart of the replanter *as* he is doing a work in replanting the church. That work involves suffering; and it is exactly in the midst of that suffering that the replanter truly knows Jesus in the "power of His resurrection and the fellowship of His sufferings" (Phil. 3:10), but the good news is that God raises the dead—including those that feel they are going to die.

Bob Bickford is a replanting pastor, National Replanting Catalyst with the North American Mission Board, Chair of the Church Revitalization Team of the St. Louis Metro Baptist Association, and founder of Churchreplanters.com

Dave

We start 1200 churches a yr
We close 900.

Churches that die:
1. Tend to rely on programs
2.   "   "   "   " personalities
3. Resent the community for not
   responding as they responded
4. Value process of the decision
   over outcome of the decision
   (lack of trust)
5. Value their preferences over the
   needs of the unreached.
   Make disciples who can make
   disciples who can change
   the community.
6. Inability to pass meaningful
   leadership to the next generation
7. Cease to gradually become part
   of the community
8. Soothe pain of death w/
   projects

Love, preach, pray & stay

NOTES

1. The SBC realizes twelve hundred to thirteen hundred new churches each year.

2. John Piper, *Let the Nations Be Glad!* 2nd ed. (Grand Rapids, MI: Baker Academic, 2003), 17.

3. Author heard Ed Stetzer say this phrase many times in several different settings.

4. Erwin McManus, *An Unstoppable Force: Daring to Be the Church God Had in Mind* (Colorado Springs, CO: David C. Cook, 2013), 34.

ABOUT THE AUTHOR

Mark Clifton is a pastor, church planter, church revitalizer, mission strategist, coach, and mentor to young leaders. He has planted numerous churches throughout North America and most recently replanted a dying urban core church in Kansas City, Missouri. Additionally, Mark has served as a regional and national leader for church planting and missions. Currently Mark serves as the Senior Director of Replanting at the North American Mission Board of the Southern Baptist Convention

He and his wife Jill live in Shawnee, Kansas.